WHO OWNS SCOTLAND NOW?

Who Owns Scotland Now?
THE USE AND ABUSE OF PRIVATE LAND

Auslan Cramb

MAINSTREAM
PUBLISHING
EDINBURGH AND LONDON

First published in Great Britain in 1996 by
MAINSTREAM PUBLISHING COMPANY (EDINBURGH) LTD
7 Albany Street
Edinburgh EH1 3UG

ISBN 1 84018 321 7

A catalogue record for this book is available from the British Library

Typeset in Berkeley Book and Cheltenham

Printed and bound in Finland by WS Bookwell Ltd

To Catriona

CONTENTS

PREFACE

M y father worked for the Forestry Commission and remembers John McEwen well. He once visited the tireless socialist and forester in his garden shed at Blairgowrie and found him poring over countless maps in the act of preparing *Who Owns Scotland?*, the controversial account of land-owning published in 1977.

At the time of its publication, I was a geography student at Aberdeen University and unaware of the 'great debate' on land-ownership, far less McEwen's calls for the nationalisation of land. Indeed, I was barely aware of land-owning itself.

Until the age of nine, I had lived in Glennachulish and was used to being taken on to Rannoch Moor or into Commission forests to walk or fish. The mountains appeared free and fine. It was much later that I learned something which was not taught in my geography degree – that the Highlands are a seriously damaged landscape.

I have never tired of visiting Argyll, Wester Ross, Caithness, Sutherland and the Hebrides. But they no longer seem to me the wholly mystical places to which I once reacted emotionally and uncomprehendingly, in the way that so many visitors, and resident Scots, still do.

It remains a thrill to be on Loch Maree, or to walk on Letterewe estate, but I can never be in such places, or even drive up the too-familiar A9, through Drumochter pass, without a sense of frustration at how different it might be.

I have been in Norwegian forests and in regenerating woodlands in Scotland, and I have seen landscapes where people and nature are closer together. I do believe Scotland's wild lands could be infinitely more magical, productive and welcoming.

Some of John McEwen's words today seem intemperate and rude. But he was expressing genuine concern about the state of Scotland, and I hope I am doing the same.

My own book is born out of nothing more than a belief that change for the better can yet happen. It is a belief which is gaining currency. Even among those who own great tracts of bare land.

INTRODUCTION

The Worst of Types, the Best of Types

L et's accentuate, meantime, the negative. Landowners can be arrogant, ignorant and patronising. They can be viewed as anachronistic, remarkable dinosaurs ravaging the Scottish landscape long after their like has become extinct elsewhere. Why, oh why – the more flamboyant might ask – was there never a Scottish Revolution?

Landowners in this country have, in many cases, survived by power, patronage, and by marrying into other landed families. They have been courted by, and have courted, successive governments, and they continue to exercise power beyond reason on thousands of people and hundreds of communities throughout Scotland.

Yet they often have neither the funds, nor the desire, to manage the land in a way which would benefit the local people and the local environment. They can know their own land intimately and remain extraordinarily oblivious to the ongoing environmental change – that is to say, degradation – taking place on it. They may know next to nothing about the processes of woodland regeneration, nothing of the creeping erosion of centuries and the damage to mountain heath. They do not understand that their fathers, and their fathers' fathers, have been part of the same process.

In blissful, or wilful, ignorance, across the wide swathe of the

Highlands stretching from the Angus glens in the south-east to the wild lands of north-west Sutherland, they retain the pre-Victorian institution of the sporting estate, a much-criticised form of management which succeeds only in satisfying the narrow interests of those who want to shoot or catch animals for fun. In almost all cases, the individual estate makes little or no money, and is maintained – as it was set up in the last century – for the pleasure of man. (It is invariably men who covet and derive pleasure from great tracts of land.)

The landed are part of a self-perpetuating élite, educated at Eton/Harrow and Oxford/Cambridge, pursuing careers in London. They eschew the Scottish education system, thereby preserving the problems associated with the clash of types in the Highlands – the absentee owner with the posh accent and a confidence which comes across as arrogance, and the diffident local who may feel he knows the place better. And again, such a system perpetuates the outdated view of much of Scotland as a sort of personal, sporting paradise; a backyard for the members of White's and Pratt's in which to play country games.

The estates – with the exception of the often verdant policy woodlands around the big house – are characterised by brown hills bereft of woodland. Many Scots assume the bare hills are natural. In fact, they are scenes of man-made dereliction, of declining biodiversity, of dwindling wildlife. They are good for the fox and the crow, because of the amount of carrion provided by dead sheep and deer, and the high tops still support rare summer visitors like the dotterel, but much of the land is strangely quiet. Sightings of red deer are very common; sightings of characteristic birds of prey, of moorland birds, of otters, badgers, pine martens, or wildcats are extremely rare.

Statistics show that the animals associated with environmental damage – the red deer, the grey squirrel and the mink – are increasing, while 12 of the country's 48 land mammals are declining, along with dozens of species of birds and plants.

Even where the owner is the latest issue of a landed family which has owned an estate for 600 years, it makes little difference. Integrated management is still lacking. Commonly, the day-to-day running of the big house and the moor is left to a professional factor who is rarely better equipped than his distant employer to manage on a sound basis.

Meanwhile, for all of the twentieth century and most of the nineteenth, over the area of Scotland thought of as land-owning territory – just about everywhere on lower grade land north and south of the central belt – the extractive regimes continue. Benefiting the owner, failing the environment, doing little for the local community.

The combination of sheep-farming, deerstalking and grouse-shooting (particularly where muir burning is badly controlled) continues to remove vitality from the very soil which was created through thousands of years by the birch, oak and pine woods which should be the real resource, the real source of wealth for the Highlands and Islands. Yet how many estate owners manage their land from the point of view of the soil and the water? It is the soil and vegetation which are the basis of any land-use system, and it is the soil and vegetation which have been exploited for millennia, most avidly in the last 200 years, in much of Scotland.

Grazing animals are kept in numbers far beyond the carrying capacity of the land and as a result there is no, or little, regeneration of those native pine, birch or oak woods. Pines which raised their heads above the heather in the middle of the eighteenth century (as they did on Mar Lodge estate in the Cairngorms) have seen no new recruits to the forest since that date.

In many areas, the biological potential of the land is displayed only on islands which are covered with a positively luxuriant, almost obscene, growth, in comparison with the brown edges of the loch and the bare heather or coarse grass landscapes which stretch away across the hills. These bare hills – many of them in the west Highlands denuded of heather by bad burning practices to improve the ground for sheep and deer – are the so-called deer forests. In some areas, the salmon and sea trout of the rivers are the game which have been exploited.

What has happened to the sporting quarry over the years? Grouse have disappeared from 70 per cent of their natural range at the beginning of the twentieth century, salmon and sea trout numbers are in decline, while red deer numbers have more than doubled, from

150,000 to 350,000, between the 1960s and 1980s. We need more migratory fish; we need far fewer deer.

Many of the native woodland remnants – the living banks of nutrients and insects which feed other life forms – have disappeared or are fast deteriorating. More than 30 flowering plants have become extinct since 1930, 26 lichens have disappeared this century and many more are in decline.

Landowners (having learned as much ignorance in their youth) tend to be dismissive of the 'birch scrub' which they imagine once covered much of the poorer land, or the peat bogs which they were told were unproductive and barren. In fact, Scotland's raised bogs – only 9 per cent of the 850 are in near-natural condition – are odd oceans of biodiversity, supporting a wide range of plant and insect life.

Where remnants of natural habitat do survive, in ancient forest, for example, they are protected principally by the carrot of Government grants to owners who are not preserving the habitat themselves. In most cases, it suits the owner to keep too many deer on the land, or to maximise grouse numbers, because estate values are based on the game bag, the number of stags or grouse shot. Hardly surprising, then, that there is no real concern about the continuing destruction of a great, but barely surviving, habitat – the Caledonian pine forest which provides a link with ancient Scotland. The same illogicality applies in other parts of the world: the Sami people in northern Norway reckon their wealth by the number of reindeer they own. Such practices make conservation impossible.

Then, to complete the scene of a countryside in recession, add to the failures of private estate management the failures of post-war forestry. These swathes of single-species, single-age trees, so despised by the Prince of Wales, were created with discredited downhill ploughing (which still happens). The practice helped pour damaging fertilisers into the rivers, it garnered acid pollution from the atmosphere, silted up the salmon redds with valuable soil washed off the land and worked to destroy what little biodiversity of life may have survived in the mountains and moors. Commercial forests were planned with no regard to the river systems, neighbouring land, deer herds or birdlife, and provide only limited benefit to local communities. No integration, although favourable forestry tax regimes (since largely removed) helped landowners make money.

In all of this chaotic scene there is no financial measurement of environmental well-being, no environment audit in the planning system, no premium for the sight of a golden eagle or a peregrine falcon during the grouse drive, no recompense for the glory of the aspen or the rowan on the hill, no future – in Lapland – for the reindeer-eating wolverine, or in Scotland for the persecuted hen harrier which preys on grouse.

And while landowners and their factors lambast poachers and complain that sheriff courts hand out the lightest of sentences, the gamekeeper goes on blithely poisoning, shooting and trapping protected birds of prey.

Anything else? Well, if money does accrue from what survives of Scotland's natural heritage, it accrues to the pocket of the individual, who may make his money selling bathrooms or growing tea. It does not go directly to the local population, however paternalistic the laird.

The estate will argue that it is an engine of production and job creation, that shooting, for example, provides jobs for 12,000 people and a total revenue (in 1988–89) of £29 million, that the total sporting income for the Scottish economy in 1990 was £44 million. Such figures, however, do not reveal the level of subsidy poured into these estates in one way or another, and say nothing of the alternatives which might exist in a healthier environment. Estates of 50,000 acres commonly provide direct employment for no more than a handful of people, on some of the lowest salaries in Britain. After all, as the land is maintained for pleasure, it is hardly likely to be run at considerable expense, never mind maximum efficiency.

Landowners, all the same, will complain that Europe is introducing unwelcome and unnecessary restrictions, that green groups exaggerate the problems, that subsidies are too low or too difficult to come by, that death duties have crippled many a fine estate enterprise.

They will complain that where there are crofts on the land, the crofters tend to be difficult, can buy their crofts, enjoy low rents and have guaranteed access to the common grazings of the hill. All of which is true and begs the question, why keep the crofting lands? The answer – in order to have the sporting rights and, perhaps, to boast of ownership of many thousands of Highland acres.

Yet the privileged crofters cannot decide to plant trees without the landowner's permission, cannot exploit water resources, cannot rent out fishing, and cannot shoot one of the too-numerous deer for the pot, unless the animal is supping in the vegetable patch.

In short, landowners retain powers today, and have pretensions, which are unreasonable, even dangerous.

Most of the above is true. As a rollicking criticism of the Scottish landowner and the state of much of our poorer hill land, it is not far off the mark. It is not, after all, unusual to hear people lay the blame for all of Scotland's environmental or social ills in the countryside at the door of the laird. Sweeping statements, of course, rarely paint a complete picture. It would, in truth, be preposterous to blame landowners alone for the state of the Scottish environment. Some Labour politicians may peddle this line, and some Scottish newspapers love to hate the rich dukes and lords who have the audacity to seek public funding for works on their land.

But there must, I believe, be more to the current interest in land-owning issues than a simple laird-bashing exercise. It has been said that there is a reawakening of popular concern over the role and status of the landowner in Scotland, that books such as this are an example of that concern, of a bubbling debate. I am not convinced that there is a popular unrest now about the feudal state of affairs we have inherited in Scottish land tenure, any more than there was in 1977 when the late John McEwen published the intemperate work, *Who Owns Scotland?*, which called for nothing less than full-scale land nationalisation.

Sure enough, the Labour Government has brought with it long-awaited land reform legislation that will restore a measure of involvement in land issues to those who live and work the land, as opposed to those who own it. Inevitably, these developments have excited media interest and raised the profile of the land-owning question. It is, after all, being debated in the Scottish Parliament. Yet the subject remains the preserve of a small number of radically minded campaigners, and a few committed politicians.

There has been no sudden realisation among the public of the problems associated with who owns Scotland; there is no demand on the streets for the feudal system to be swept away, although swept away it will be.

However, the land reform legislation made possible by Scotland's first parliament for 300 years has been a wake-up call for the lairds. The Scottish Landowners' Federation has tried, for the first time, to engage in reasonable debate with its enemies. It has attempted to woo the press, and it has acknowledged that some degree of reform is inevitable and necessary. It did not, for example, strongly object to the disappearance of the anachronistic feudal system that allows landowners to exercise arcane powers over people who own their homes.

Some landowners have put their heads above the parapet to defend their practices – no bad thing – and to offer positive suggestions. Some have retreated into caricature to live out the last days of the Raj.

In fact, the landowners have had little to fear so far from land reform. The only radical step taken so far by the Scottish Executive is the 'right-to-buy' legislation that will allow communities to purchase land when it is offered for sale. The community must register an interest while the land is in private hands and if the owner decides to sell an independent valuer will set the price. All the community has to do is prove that it is serious about ownership, and raise the necessary cash. It will then get the land for the going price, regardless of any larger offer on the table.

Radical? Well, reasonably so. The lairds claim it amounts to interference in the market, but they could have had it much worse. For example, 25 per cent of all estates in Scotland will not be affected by the legislation for the reason that they have been held by the same families for over 400 years. At present, there are few communities in rural Scotland with the will to take on land ownership. The changes will be slow. Meanwhile, landowners will do their cause a great deal of good, and may avoid further radical steps, if they try to work with the new situation.

More of this later. Let's develop the 'rollicking criticism'. Who are

Scotland's lairds, and what is expected of them? They are, archetypically, the bulbous-nosed, tweed-class gents who do still exist. But they are also pension funds, insurance companies, environment groups, rock stars, crooks and foreign aristocrats. The diversity of owners is increasing, along with the range of interests which motivate them. Some are good, some have yet to prove themselves, many are bad.

The qualifications? Well, the next big laird could be you or me. The privilege and power that comes with the position requires just one qualification, and that is a large wallet. If you have the money, you can buy 50,000 Highland acres, with a mansion house, two or three employees, several holiday cottages, mountains, heather and deer aplenty.

Your nationality does not matter – never mind that you are not allowed to buy large areas of land in your own country, or neighbouring countries. It does not matter that you have no intention of living on the land, or that you visit it for no more than two or three weeks in the stag-stalking season – despite the fact that in your own country you cannot buy land unless you spend most of the year in residence on the property.

The existing form of management does not have to be maintained, neither do the loyal estate staff. You do not have to win the approval of the locals – they have no say in the sale of the land which surrounds them.

There may be an agreement on areas of conservation importance – remnant woodlands for example – but there is no need to renew the arrangement when it is due for review with the official agency. In fact, until recently, if you had a designated conservation area on your estate, say a boggy site of special scientific interest, you could threaten to cover it with trees and be paid large sums of money in order not to. Yes, you could be paid for doing nothing. John Cameron in Glen Lyon, the former chairman of ScotRail, made more than one million pounds by threatening to plant trees.

In addition, there is no need to identify yourself to the public when you are in the process of buying 50,000 acres, even if these include a national nature reserve. You could be a great train robber, or the laird of another 100,000 acres elsewhere in Scotland. Never mind that in your own country there are strict rules and regulations on the owning of land. And, if you grow tired of the place, there is no need to hold on to it. You can sell it again within weeks. You might even break it up, selling a bit here, a bit there in order to make money.

Occasionally, you will be asked by local people if you can spare a plot for a private house, but there is no need to oblige. You can assume (unless you are a particularly high-minded and liberal individual) that you have no particular responsibility to consider the local population and its economy – although you will be able to increase the rents of your tenants every few years. You can, if you want, use your land entirely for the enjoyment of yourself and your friends. You need contribute nothing to the economy of Scotland: you might bring your own cook, food and equipment with you. On the other hand, you can influence the cultural, economic and physical environment around you. And as forestry and agriculture are not part of the planning process, you can do pretty much what you want along these lines.

Under Labour's access reforms, you will have to admit that people are allowed to walk on your land. But you can probably still get away with putting up sings warning unwelcome visitors that high velocity rifles are in use during the long winter stalking season. You can still employ rude stalkers who are gruff and unhelpful to walkers and climbers, and you can still put padlocks on estate gates and allow shelters to fall into ruin. You are not obliged to maintain the paths and tracks used by the unwashed public and there is nothing to stop you putting up 'no camping' signs wherever you fancy. You can also, if you are particularly bloody-minded, accuse visitors of being unreasonable and of disrupting estate activity. They are unlikely to come back.

And here is something else to your advantage. You will find that you have joined a small, but influential, club. The Scottish Landowners' Federation has around 4,000 members, and you and your new friends will own 80 per cent of the land. You might want to invite a government minister up for a spot of shooting. Those Labour and Liberal Democrat types may talk tough for the cameras but, like everyone else, they enjoy good claret and a spot of fine country living. You might also entertain the senior executives of Scottish Natural Heritage and, if you are a youngish and active laird, you might want to join one of the nature agency boards where you can keep an eye on some of the more insane environmental restrictions proposed for you and your colleagues.

You will, of course, face the occasional piece of unwelcome legislation. But at least you can be assured that the Conservative Party and the right-wing press will spring to your defence. You will find you are not complete bereft of friends in the liberal New Scotland.

All in all, buying land in Scotland is not a bad bet if you fancy owning your own kingdom, albeit one that can be wet and ridden by midges. But remember, only those with a large wallet need apply.

That this situation survives in quite the way it does is due to the fact that Scotland is one of the few countries in which, until recently, there had been no period of land reform. The only historical challenge to the landowners was the passing of the Crofters Holding Act of 1886, the move which ended the Clearances, and which so incensed the Duke of Argyll that he resigned from the Cabinet. The laird's power has not suffered much since.

In the 1970s, forester and socialist McEwen (*Who Owns Scotland?*) waxed vitriolic. He wrote of the 'tragic' state of the land, he said the entire 10,000,000 acres of rough grazing in Scotland were suffering from bad management, and he admitted his aim was to 'show up the stranglehold of landlords and have it smashed'. He bemoaned the 'half a million splendid acres' behind castle walls which were not used for agriculture – for example, the attractive parks or policies which still surround Blair Castle today. Little legislation was imposed on owners, he said, and lairds were arrogant and mean.

His solution was to be delivered in three stages. First, there would be a land register established, second, there would be a Land Commission overseeing land management, and, finally, all land would be nationalised.

Some of his ideas are only just being realised. While a land register has existed in Norway, Sweden, Denmark, Holland, France, Germany and Switzerland for some time, it is only now being put in place in Scotland. And other small sates control the way in which land is bought and sold, without being called xenophobic or discriminatory – as opponents of foreign ownership in Scotland often are.

And here is the single great flaw in the unique Scottish system – it allows anyone from anywhere in the world to buy huge areas of land and then fails to decree what can and cannot happen on the land. Land ownership – and therefore land management – is a lottery.

When Glenfeshie estate in the Cairngorms – part of a so-called national nature reserve, which is a disgrace by most international standards – was sold in 1994, there was one individual from the Far East who wanted to buy it in order to farm the deer antlers which would be ground down and turned into an aphrodisiac. If he had come up with the money, he would have succeeded.

As a commodity, Scottish land is subject to the fashions, fads and the relative health of world economics. There has been an Arab period, there has been a Dutch period, there is an ongoing Danish period – some foreign nationals actually get tax breaks by moving their money 'offshore' and buying land in Scotland – and there was a very strong Hong Kong period, in which ex-patriots bought up estates and mansions in order to retire in 1997.

There was a domestic period of purchase in the 1980s during the London money market boom and the era of the yuppie when, imitating Victorian fashion, it was the ultimate status symbol to have a Highland sporting estate. Many of those yuppies have since lost their money, and their estates, as easily as they came by them. There was even a rock group period when Paul McCartney, Genesis, and Ian Anderson of Jethro Tull all got in on the land-owning scene.

Put crudely, the largest landowners are still the traditional families, but foreign ownership continues apace. Much of Wester Ross is Dutch, Argyll is part-owned by Danes and Belgians, and there are Arabs in Easter Ross and Perthshire. In addition, environment ownership is increasing through purchases by groups, including the John Muir Trust, the Royal Society for the Protection of Birds and the National Trust for Scotland. Land agents would have us believe that private owners today have a more holistic view, are as much concerned about the brown argus butterfly and the twinflower as the bag of grouse and the number of eagles preying on precious game. Maybe.

It is an alluring prospect. Just look at the glossy sales brochures of staggering mountain and river scenery, count the places at the dining-room table, work out the income from the holiday cottages and staff houses on the land, imagine the thrill as you roll up the drive in the Range Rover, or walk home off the hill, a royal stag slung across the back of the pony and the stalker carrying your rifle. All for the cost of a few square feet of office space in London.

You might use the place to clinch business deals. You might use it to entertain your friends, or your mistress. You might, as John Kluge (of Metromedia Inc, ninth richest man in the world) did, buy an estate in order to allow your new wife (half your age) to live next to the royals at Balmoral. You can do this with Scottish land.

The question – who are the landowners? – has significance because, just as there is a lack of knowledge among the populace about matters rural, there is an ignorance of who owns what. And there is an obvious reason for this. People have been able to buy land for its privacy value, precisely because there has been no detailed land register.

There is the Register of Sasines, but you do not have to have your purchase recorded there, and, if you do, you do not have to disclose the size of the estate or the price you paid. Even if the information is placed there by your solicitor, then discovering the information still involves a member of the public in a personal visit to Edinburgh, a fee of £5 (£25 if you make the inquiry by telephone), and a lot of hanging around for something which just may not exist.

Scottish politicians of socialist or nationalist tendencies have long called for a proper register. In 1979, an Act was passed establishing a halfway house: there is a Land Register in preparation (it has been in preparation for 17 years) which includes all sales. But it is not retrospective. Under the Scottish Executive's land reform legislation, a more detailed national database may be set up to fill in the gaps, such as an up-to-date name and address for every estate owner. Landowners remain, in a sense, shareholders in Scotland with executive powers but no accountability.

There are many examples of the follies visited on our land. There was the Swiss businessman Gerard Panchaud, who bought not one huge estate, but three. He began in 1961 with Mar Lodge in the Cairngorms and went on to buy Ammuinsuidhe on Harris – one with its bizarre mock-Georgian manor, the other with its solid Victorian castle – and Tulchan on Speyside. His intention was to provide a level of luxury accommodation never seen in Scotland for those people who enjoy shooting deer and catching fish. His wilder ideas for Mar Lodge included a ski development and an airport.

He was attempting the near impossible, however, he was trying to make traditional sporting management provide a profit. There are no more than a handful of sporting estates which make money, and those that do often rely on good salmon-fishing to spread their income from February to October. The estates which rely on deer – the majority of them – hope to make enough money in seven weeks to support the staff for the rest of the year.

Luckily, Panchaud's farfetched plans for Mar Lodge were turned down. Yet he did quite nicely. Having bought Mar Lodge for under £100,000 in 1967, he sold it for nearly £7 million in 1989, thanks to Patricia Kluge, the former soft-porn star turned tycoon's wife (of whom, more later). All this on an estate which has been described by Prince Charles as the single most important area of land in Britain for nature conservation, an area which has been damaged by the prevailing management policy for the past 250 years. The Harris estate was sold by Panchaud's widow to Jonathan Bulmer of cider fame. She retained, however, the area earmarked as a possible site for a coastal superquarry – the one bit of the land which might make money.

Then there is His Excellency Mahdi Mohammed Al Tajir, the Arab owner of Blackford Estate near Stirling, and the producer of Highland Spring mineral water, who has indulged in 'latter-day clearances', and who refuses to carry out any improvements on parts of his land or to release any houses for let or sale; there are the Italians on Loch Ericht-side who visit for a few weeks and do nothing for the rest of the year; there is the Arab on the west coast whose only instruction to his factor was 'make sure you don't make any money'; and there is the Englishman in the Cairngorms who boasts that he had 64 buzzards killed in one year.

There is – there always is – a case for the defence, even if it is not the greatest concern of this book. Traditional owners have kept land in the same family for hundreds of years and that can be a good thing. The places where people want to walk today – and can walk, by and large – are private estates. Many estate policies and hills are far more attractive than farmland, and far more accessible. Paths have not been maintained at all in many lowland agricultural areas and the interesting, boggy, wet places have been drained and turned to pasture.

And if landowners in the Highlands and the Borders are to a great extent responsible for the way the land looks today, and if people like it – and they do – then some would argue that they should be congratulated for it. There are estates like Rothiemurchus in the Cairngorms, owned by the Grant family for many centuries, which retain very beautiful woodland environments. The same can be said for parts of Buccleuch estate in the Borders, and even parts of Atholl in Perthshire.

Landowners do contribute to the local economy through their employment of staff and their management of the land for sport: there is also a spin-off benefit to hotels and guest houses and pubs and specialist shops. In some cases, benevolent owners provide good, and astonishingly cheap, housing to their workers (and retired staff), and may try to let properties to young families. They may also invest or participate in the local community in a significant way. Feudalism, although anachronistic, is not automatically bad for the estate worker.

And, oddly, in the matter of investment, the incoming foreign laird may be preferable to the old survivors. There are examples throughout Scotland of largesse by Europe's business millionaires who have fallen in love with, and bought, their own bit of Scotland. Paul van Vlissingen at Letterewe helped build the local swimming-pool, John Kluge refurbished Mar Lodge staff houses to generous standards.

Anyone, of course, can be a bad landowner. Even environment or community owners can abuse the ground. And this obvious truth points again to the need for the proper incentives, controls and subsidies. What the owner is obliged to do with his land is almost as important as the nature of the ownership itself.

THE WORST OF TYPES, THE BEST OF TYPES

Many environmental problems exist today because of Forestry Commission policy, because of headage payments for sheep and because of the presence, or absence, of integrated planning which considers natural heritage interests as paramount.

We should ask, what is it that we want from the land? If, for example, the answer is that we want more benefit and control to accrue to local communities, and less to individuals, then there is room for improvement. If we want the land to achieve something nearer its full biological potential, then there is enormous room for improvement. If we believe that vast swathes of the Highlands could be doing more than growing sheep, deer and grouse, or if we think that natural environments are preferable to degraded environments, then there is vast room for improvement.

The landowner and the land-owning system has a major role to play in this, as has the political system. If we do not want one grouse moor to merge into another *ad infinitum*, then it is possible for an enlightened Scottish Executive to do more than tinker with land reform. And it is possible for the public to precipitate this.

Far from recognising any great public concern on such issues, I would suggest there is not enough public concern. There should be an outcry about the rotten state of the Scottish rural environment, social and natural. Changes in who owns the land, and how it is managed, must be part of our future development if we are to avoid creating something akin to the rocky (man-made) moonscapes of Iceland.

At the simplest level, it must be wrong that so much of Scotland is run at an annual loss by rich men who can afford to subsidise country sports. It is undeniable that sporting estates fail to make money for their owners, and therefore are starved of investment. Might there be a more useful way to manage our land?

Change does not mean sweeping away the existing land-owning system, but certainly it means introducing more prescription, abandoning – in many cases – the voluntary principle and replacing it with hard rules and regulations. Some such changes are suggested later in this book, and they can be made with the co-operation of landowners or against their will.

Undoubtedly, it will be a bit of both.

The Top Twenty Landowners in Scotland?

		Acres
1	Forestry Commission	1,600,000
2	Duke of Buccleuch/Lord Dalkeith Four estates in the Borders	270,000
3	Scottish Executive Rural Affairs Department Ninety per cent crofting land	260,000
4	National Trust for Scotland Includes 75,000-acre Mar Lodge	190,000
5	Alcan Highland Estate Land used for electricity generation	135,000
6	Blair charitable Trust, Sarah Troughton Estates around Dunkeld/Blair Atholl	130,000
7	Capt. Alwyn Farquharson Invercauld on Deeside/Smaller estate, Argyll	125,000
8	Duchess of Westminster, Lady Mary Grosvenor	120,000

Grosvenor Sporting Estates, Sutherland

9 Earl of Seafield   105,000
    Seafield estates, Speyside

10 Crown Estate Commission   100,000
    Three main estates, including Glenlivet

11 Edmund Vestey and four sons   100,000
    Assynt, mountain property

12 South Uist Estate Co. (syndicate)   92,000
    Sporting estate with 900 crofts

13 Sir Donald Cameron of Lochiel, and family   90,000
    Sporting/forestry centred on Achnacarry Castle

14 Countess of Sutherland, Lord Strahnaver   90,000
    Sporting estates in Sutherland

15 Royal society for the Protection of Birds   87,400
    Fifty-two separate reserves

16 Paul van Vlissingen   87,000
    Letterewe 'wilderness', West Ross

17 Scottish Natural Heritage   84,400
    Nature reserves

18 Robin Fleming and family   80,000
    Blackmount/Glen Etive

19 Hon. Chas. Pearson   77,000
    Dunecht

20 Lord Margadale   73,000
    Islay

Most private estates are held in trust. The list, however, identifies the main beneficiaries and families behind the key estates. The acreages were, in most cases, supplied by the owners, and may not accord with detailed map-based calculations.

MAJOR FOREIGN LANDOWNERS (NOT ALREADY LISTED)

		Acres
1	Unknown Malaysian businessman (Andras company)	70,000
	Glenavon, Cairngorms (40,000)	
	also Braulen, Inverness-shire (30,000)	
2	Mohammed bin Raschid al Maktoum, Arab billionaire	63,000
	Glomach, West Benula, Inverinate, Wester Ross	
3	Kjeld Kirk-Christiansen, head of Lego, Denmark	50,000
	Strathconon, Mid Ross	
4	Profs. Joseph and Lisbet Koerner, Swedish Tetra Pak heiress	
	Corrour, Lochaber	48,000
5	Stanton Avery, US billionaire	30,000
	Dunbeath, Caithness	
6	Mohammed Al Fayed, owner of Harrods	30,000
	Balnagowan, Ross and Cromarty	
7	Urs Schwarzenberg, Swiss businessman	26,000
	Ben Alder, Inverness-shire	
8	Count Knuth, Danish aristocrat	20,000
	Ben Loyal, Sutherland	
9	His Excellency Mahdi Mohammed Al Tajir,	20,000
	United Arab Emirates	
	Blackford, Perthshire	
10	Prof. Ian Roderick Macneil of Barra, American clan chief	
	Barra and islands	17,200
11	Eric Delwart, Belgian	16,000
	Kilchoan, Knoydart	
12	Lucan Ardenberg, Dane	10,000
	Pitmain, Inverness-shire	

13 Fred Olsen, Norwegian shipping magnate   4,000
    Forest Estate, Galloway
14 Dr Sybrand and Feya Heerma van Voss, Dutch   4,000
    Blar a' Chaoruinn, Fort William
15 Hans Depre, Belgian businessman   4,000
    Clova, near Lumsden, Aberdeenshire

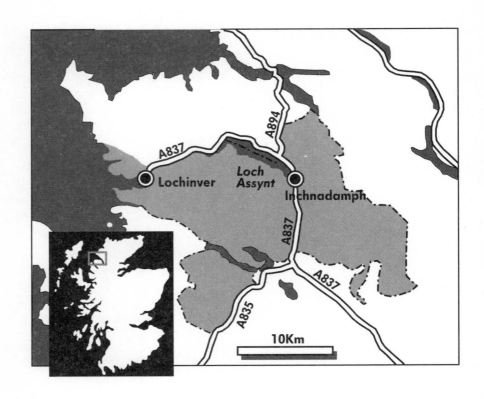

ACREAGE – 100,000
OWNER – EDMUND VESTEY AND FOUR SONS
MANAGED FOR – DEERSTALKING, SALMON-FISHING
POINTS OF INTEREST – RARE AGREEMENT PROVIDES
EXEMPTION FROM INHERITANCE TAX

CHAPTER ONE

Assynt Estate

I have always loved the village of Contin for its frontier qualities. It is not so much the place itself but the fact that it is on the border: you enter the village in the fertile east and by the time you have crossed a tributary of the Conon you are in the longed-for embrace of the west. You enter with the road cutting between farm fields, and you leave in an avenue of birch and broom. By the time you have travelled the extra few miles to Garve, there can be no doubt. The hilltops in March are bare and brown, the house fires smoke all day, and the Garve Hotel has been dipped in a hideous shade of pink, designed to catch bus-bound tourists of the Barbara Cartland tendency. If the hotels are hellish, then you must be in the Highlands. (This is a useful generalisation, but one which I cannot honestly apply to the Garve Hotel, as I have never set foot in it.)

There is a sign in Contin offering a simple choice between North and West. Invariably, I take the latter road, which opens up the true west Highlands and options ranging from Mallaig through Lochcarron to Torridon, Loch Maree, Gairloch, Ullapool, Kinloch-bervie and even far-flung Tongue.

On the road I am following, the North and West choice is next offered 90 minutes later, north Ullapool. By which time the familiar barren heath slopes are well established and the visitor might imagine the landscape had not changed for a millennium or more. But if you care to look closely, there are signs of another history, or a different future.

When you have climbed out of Ullapool and dropped down to the sea again you can look west to Isle Martin – a drab view on this snowy March day – which was once the centre of the Scottish herring industry. Its message is not obvious in early spring when the leaves have fallen from the birch, but there are trees on Isle Martin, planted by Bernard and Emma Planterose and friends, the local nurserymen who have been proving that you can grow trees on soil enriched by seaweed and even by human waste, and that today's acid highland soil, resting on some of the oldest rocks on the world, is not yet entirely past it. In summer you would need binoculars to see Isle Martin's green leaf. And when you walk among the woods which are no more than 13 years old, the transformation in the local micro-environment is astonishing.

From even a close distance, the enclosed area is not so impressive. But 12ft and 15ft birch and willow and rowan are tall enough to create a real woodland effect when you are among them, particularly when there are berries on the trees and birds are singing. The wood is laced and tangled with brambles, brought here by bird droppings and now thriving on the hillside – 'craw-planted', as the old expression goes.

The place is redolent of rural harvest: it offers berries for jam and pies and wine, mushrooms for cooking; it offers shelter to man and animal; it offers wood for fences, for a walking stick, for the fire. Eventually it will offer much more.

But I am on the A837 today, heading north over slush-covered roads, passing a sign declaring that the traveller has entered Assynt. This is the point where Ross-shire gives way to Sutherland. Not so long ago, Assynt was owned by the Duke of Sutherland, then by the Duke of Westminster. For the past 60 years it has been owned by the family behind the Vestey Group, the London shipping and food conglomerate. Edmund Vestey inherited from his father, and has in turn handed on parts of the estate, and his love for the place, to his four sons. They spend a month or two in the area every year.

Here, just when the traveller has been convinced once again that trees have been banished and that human habitation must never have thrived, there appears the ruin of Ardvreck Castle on the shore of Loch Assynt. In the snow-mantled scene it looks like a crazy place for a fortress, a meaningless choice for a settlement, far less a stronghold. But under the snow the grass is greener here, thanks to a limestone outcrop and generations of work by crofters. There once was a hardy population on the shores of this loch.

The castle, sadly unkempt today, is famed as the place where the Duke of Montrose, after many famous battles fighting to keep the Stuarts on the throne, was captured by the McLeods of Assynt and sent to Edinburgh to be executed. He sought shelter in the castle, where he was betrayed. If you have time to stop, you can find the remains of the houses nearby.

The shores of Loch Assynt are also famed for their fascinating geology, which in 1926 gave up one of Scotland's most important archaeological sites. The Inchnadamph caves were found to contain bones of reindeer, lynx, wolf and bear. It is hard to imagine the richness of the environment which must have supported great predators like the bear. Today, the biggest predator is the fox, and the ancient forests are remembered only by the whitened roots preserved in the peat.

Further along the road towards Lochinver, capital of Assynt, there is a surprise: several small islands covered in luxuriant heather and fine pine trees, like chunks of beard missed during a hasty shave. In fact, these pine trees were planted from native seed. But, like islands everywhere in the highland freshwater lochs, they are islands of evidence, islands of proof. Edmund Vestey plans to use the seed from these trees for tree-planting schemes on his stark, mountain land.

I am not stopping at the whitewashed estate office opposite the church in Lochinver, but carrying on into an odd territory, the land of North Lochinver, a 21,000-acre area of crofting land which was sold by Vestey for £1 million in 1989 to Scandinavian Property Services, backed by a Swedish entrepreneur. The firm went into liquidation three years later. Then, in an historic and – it seems to many – deeply symbolic move, the local crofters successfully raised the £300,000 needed to buy their own land. It may briefly have belonged to a Swede, but the crofters thought of it as Vestey land, and that made its purchase all the sweeter.

One of the men with the vision to make the dream happen, Bill Ritchie of the Assynt Crofters Trust, summed up in a BBC television programme the momentous nature of the achievement. 'For the first time ever, the crofters could get up in the morning and say, this is ours. And that was a huge, magnificent feeling.'

There has been no miraculous transformation of the land, but many important steps have been taken. The crofters applied for, and won approval for, their own small-scale hydro-electric scheme. They could not have done so as tenants. They applied for, and were granted funding for, new forestry on the land. They would have had to ask the landowner's permission in the past. They have let the lodge on the estate to a computer software company, not to visiting sportsmen. And they are developing the wonderful loch trout fishing, which will bring income to the trust. Ownership of the land, with all its attendant burdens, is vitally important.

The purchase by the crofters is to some extent misunderstood by urban Scots. Certainly, their achievement did create what the writer Jim Hunter calls an 'incredible resonance' throughout Scotland, exemplified in east-end pubs in Glasgow where the punters threw coins into a bucket for the Assynt crofters. But the punters had a notion of a tough bunch of crofters, fighting, as their ancestors had done at the end of the last century, for their rights, for better conditions. Fighting to be free of the awful yoke of the laird. The fact that such empathy was wrung from Scots who rarely articulate any sentiment over the Clearances was in itself significant enough; there is subconscious resentment in many of us yet. After all, many of those living in Glasgow today are descended from cleared crofters.

Yet the truth is invariably more prosaic. The Assynt crofters succeeded because there were a few individuals in that community with vision, foresight, dreams of what might be achieved. Bill Ritchie, Allan Macrae and John MacKenzie were not the norm in crofting communities, and without them the victory would not have been won. There is not a great reserve of radical crofters on this peninsula north of Lochinver, but ordinary crofters – elderly women in many cases – who were led and who were prepared to follow. Apart from another crofter purchase at Borve on Skye, and the likelihood of new crofting ownership at Melness in Sutherland, where the owner in October 1995 offered the land to his tenants free of charge, there has been no collapse of the floodgates. These vital individuals are missing from so many crofting communities, along with another deciding factor – a landowner willing to sell.

When you turn right at the entrance to Lochinver and head north on a winding coast road, like a thin strip of liquorice carelessly dropped on the landscape, you quickly see the attractions of this land to a man like Edmund Vestey, who spends his working days in a new brick building at St John's Gate in east London.

Stop at the first parking place on the left as you climb out of a depression and look back. Here is one of Scotland's great views – the panorama of Suilven, Canisp and Cul Mor. The sugar loaf, Suilven, looks just like that today in its snow shroud. All the mountain land that can be seen to the south is owned by Vestey and sons; they have assiduously sold the low land to buy more high land, concentrating – and simplifying? – their interests by owning as much as possible which is as barren as possible.

I am heading for Culkein Drumbeg (Culkein comes from the Gaelic for 'back of the head' – and there are numerous Culkeins along the way). John MacKenzie is a stalwart of the Assynt Crofters' Trust and, his house would suggest, he is no less appreciative of the landscape than Edmund Vestey. His bungalow home sits on hard rock above the Atlantic, offering fantastic sea views of Eddrachillis Bay, backed by the great saddled lump of Quinaig. There seems to be a famous hill everywhere you look in this part of Scotland.

Over rock cakes and tea, MacKenzie dismantles the Vestey reputation. 'His attitude to the place is to keep it as it is. He wants to come up here for a month in August and enjoy it as it is. He might come to the summer games occasionally. But he has no involvement whatsoever in the community. Except for resisting development.'

Resisting development is what Vestey is known best for in the Assynt croftlands, and to many inhabitants of Lochinver. MacKenzie offers a list of grievances:

♦ The community wanted a swimming-pool in Lochinver, using waste heat from the ice plant in the harbour. Vestey would not consent.

♦ Land was needed for a small factory unit development at Lochinver, but Vestey, as feudal superior, refused to grant a change of use for the council-owned site. He resisted for many years until, allegedly, threatened with adverse publicity.

♦ Vestey resisted development of the harbour, where new facilities were needed for the fishing industry.

♦ Vestey won approval for a new hotel, and a new house, on the skyline above Lochinver – 'where no one else would have succeeded'.

♦ Vestey stopped plans for a housing development by the mouth of his salmon river, the Inver.

♦ Vestey stopped plans for a tourist centre on the shore in Lochinver.

♦ Vestey's former factor acquired houses from spinsters on the estate who, their neighbours thought, should have been granted title themselves.

The list is long, varied and, depending on who you talk to, may or may not be accurate. Regardless of the accuracy, it is the view of the locals that Vestey has been a regressive landowner who may love the place, but only as an oil painting, hunting ground, and salmon reservoir. Not as a place where people live and work, and may have aspirations for new development and opportunity.

Undoubtedly, many years and more incidents have soured the relationship. There is even a fond remembrance of another landowner, Maj.Gen. William Stewart, the son of a family cleared to the nearby township of Nedd, who returned from Canada to buy Assynt and Eddrachillis from the Duke of Sutherland. When he sold it in the 1930s, the contenders were the Vesteys and the

Westminsters. The Duke of Westminster won, buying Assynt as a wedding present for a son-in-law who, as it happened, did not stay married to Lady Ursula (whose sister, Lady Mary, still lives at Kylestrome) for long. The vagaries of land deals and the marriages of the landed! The land was sold to the Vestey family at a later date.

In Assynt, as in so many other areas, the factor plays an important part in the history of the estate. MacKenzie's view of the estate, he admits, was to a large extent formed by dealing with the former factor, Peter Hay.

'Peter Hay was from Ayrshire. He was ex-army and he was a game warden in the national parks of Kenya before he came to Assynt. He treated people here as he would have done the natives in Africa. It was utterly unacceptable. He was a blustering, bombastic individual with a loud voice. His booming voice and his southern accent would engulf a shop when he entered it. People despised him.' Vestey, by contrast, is described by MacKenzie as a 'quiet, self-effacing guy'.

Slithering on the snow-covered road from picturesque Drumbeg back to Lochinver, it is possible to see some reason in Vestey's standpoint. He is not unusual in feeling he has a duty to preserve his land, and he would be quite right to be unimpressed by the scruffy caravans, held down with a mess of guy-ropes weighted with stones, which litter the croft fields in the township of Clachtoll. The vans belong to holidaymakers who pay a small annual rent to the crofters.

And then, at the entrance to Lochinver, at the top of a rise before descending into the village, there is the Glac Mhor industrial estate, an area which was once a roads depot for the regional council, and which – after much argument – was finally released from its original title conditions by Vestey, and turned into a site with several factory units. It is an unattractive advert for the village, and is the first thing seen by the visitor. But something like it was necessary, somewhere.

I am staying at the Culag Hotel on the pier, where the Wayfarer bar is full of the French trawlermen who fish out of Lochinver, catching odd-looking creatures from the deep water on the edge of the continental shelf – grenadier and black scabbard and orange roughy. The proprietor, Willie Hutchison, makes 60 per cent of his income from the bar-room commerce.

'Vestey's whole attitude,' he tells me, 'is to keep the place as a nature reserve, including the people. There was no encouragement from him, he went out of his way to stop development. Even the council had a job to get land for building houses. I can see his point of view. He bought it God knows how many years ago. In his mind he was good to the locals. Vestey was God and the people were his tenants.

'The more I see of them [the Vesteys], the more I know of them, the more I think of them as kids that have never grown up. Why are they so worried about their huge big bit of land?

'But it is the system that is bad. He is not particularly bad. He is probably quite reasonable, compared with some. The lack of development is also a terrible failure of local government which has not stood up for local people.'

Not so long ago, Hutchison's hotel was owned by Vestey. For years there had been pressure to develop the harbour area, and the landowner finally agreed to sell the land to the council, on the condition that the hotel was bulldozed. He promised to build another hotel in the village. The multi-national businessman was pre-empted, however, by the Shetlander, who bought the hotel in a back-to-back sale on the day the harbour land was sold and was granted – almost simultaneously – a licence to operate it. Vestey responded by building a hotel which he considers to be far superior.

You can see the new hotel, the Inverlodge, and Vestey's new house by its side, on the southern skyline of Lochinver. On the purple cover of the Ordnance Survey Landranger 15 map, which covers Loch Assynt and surrounding area, there is a photograph of the village, including Lochinver stores – owned and operated by Vestey's Assynt Trading Company – and, above a green and rocky ridge, the summit of Suilven crowns the scene.

If you drive to the council housing development, and the site of the successful pottery at Baddidarach, to the west of the village, you can see much the same scene. But the skyline from here is now interrupted by the protruding summit of Vestey's new house and by the barrack-like appearance (from a distance) of his hotel. This does seem to constitute a remarkable planning decision by the local authority.

It means, however, that the council tenants of Lochinver, some of whom enjoy the stunning view of Suilven, can now rejoice in looking out every day on the home of the man they are unlikely ever to meet, but who exerts a major influence on their surroundings from a plush boardroom in London.

There are two sides to every story. And perhaps the most positive development of recent years has been the retirement of the unpopular Peter Hay and the appointment of the new factor, Peter Voy. He is Scottish, he does not have a booming southern accent and he admits that the estate is 'nervous as hell' about speaking to journalists, because of the criticism the family has received in the past. He wants the estate to be even-handed in its dealings and says of Vestey and his sons: 'They genuinely do love the place. It is more than just wanting to own big chunks of land.'

The modern map of the estate is on the office wall, and reveals a ragged boundary which is the product of sales, resales, readjustments and the peccadilloes of successive owners who wanted to hang on to one corner and dispose of another. The whole is singularly mountainous. It encompasses Suilven, Canisp, Cul Mor, Benmore – its only Munro – and Inverpolly National Nature Reserve. The four forests are Inchnadamph, Drumrunie, Glencanisp and Benmore. The heartland is dominated by Glencanisp Forest – with Suilven and Canisp – which is bounded by the sea and the coastal crofting strip to the west, and by the A837 to the east and north. The land narrows to the south, missing most of Loch Sionascaig.

From the moment you pass the hamlet of Drumrunie on the A835, six miles north of Ullapool, everything you see on your left-hand side before you reach Lochinver belongs to the Vestey family. It is managed for deer, salmon and trout. Oddly, and impressively, there have been no sheep on the estate for the past ten years, but the benefit of removing one voracious grazer may be more than made up for by another.

In other estates visited for this book, I was told of stag/hind ratios of roughly one to one, as a popular ideal. And even then, natural regeneration was not possible because of grazing pressure. The last count on Assynt found 962 stags and 1,991 hinds. The annual cull is around 200 hinds, with 110 stags.

Local chat has it that the deer population seems to be bigger than ever, that deer are seen by roadsides more frequently than anyone can remember. This could be due to weather, to disturbance by hillwalkers, to the fact that sheep have been removed, to over-population and, most likely, to a combination of all four.

But here is an interesting thing. Assynt is one of the few estates in the Highlands which has a highly advantageous deal that avoids inheritance tax on the basis of the way it is managed. This deal – originally agreed with the Nature Conservancy Council, and now carried on by Scottish Natural Heritage – is largely based on the scenic quality of the place, but involves guarantees on free access being provided for the public, and sympathetic conservation management. Surely, the body responsible for the good management of Scotland's natural heritage does not endorse over-grazing on such a grand scale!

SNH is currently carrying out a detailed population and habitat survey, and Peter Voy, for one, is bracing himself for the results. 'Deer is one thing that has potential for controversy. We have no doubt that at some point they [SNH and the Red Deer Commission] will want less, and that could affect stalking.'

The estate has been divided into trusts for the four sons, who each have their area and their lodge or house. Vestey has moved out of the big house, Glancanisp, on the edge of Loch Druim Suardalain, a few miles from Lochinver, and handed it over to his eldest son.

The whole family enjoys shooting – around half the stag-shooting is let – and fishing on the three salmon rivers, the Kirkaig, the Inver and the Oykel. All of the salmon-fishing is let through the new hotel, except for the lower Inver, which is kept for the family. Grouse-shooting is no longer worth while, although Voy observes that a few family members went out in 1994 and 'shot about two and a half brace'. An odd thing to do, some would say, when so few birds survive.

The best sources of finance are sporting lets, the shop, the hotel and the filling station. Other businesses in the village have been sold, and four are rented. There are no farms on the land. The estate boasts six full-time stalkers, three full-time river watchers, three maintenance staff and part-time ghillies and watchers.

Snow seems to be following me around. Meanish, barely white flakes are beginning to swirl and fall in St John's Lane as I arrive at the appointed time at the comfortable, ultra-modern headquarters of the Vestey Group.

Worldwide, the multi-national employs around 8,000 people. The enterprises comprise food, shipping and farming, including the Blue Star shipping line, cattle and sugar ranches in Brazil, and soya, maize and cattle operations in Venezuela.

Vestey's office is comfortably furnished but cold. He has a window open behind him and I imagine the temperature is helpful to his too-ruddy complexion. With his red cheeks, slightly bulbous and highly coloured nose, he would be anybody's idea of a butcher if he donned a striped apron. Part of his business, until recently, was the Dewhurst chain of butchers.

Vestey does not appear entirely at ease; he stares for a second before answering some questions, and rarely speaks for long. He is, as I was told, a quiet guy But he accepts responsibility for the actions of his former factor, Peter Hay. It was not a case of the factor alienating the locals while the landowner was too busy elsewhere.

'I think any factor, in time, is bound to be unpopular unless he says yes to everything all the time. If he said that, he would probably be unpopular with his employer.

'From my point of view, I would think he [Peter Hay] walked a pretty skilful tightrope. There was probably a good love-hate relationship. Hay kept me aware of what was going on. He was a fairly tough character, he did not suffer fools gladly. He was not going to be pushed into various ideas that didn't make too much sense.

'I am not concerned about what we have resisted. If it is painted as having resisted measures just for the sake of resisting, I would take issue with that.'

His own examples of things he has resisted include the plan for a new tourist centre – 'to which they wanted me to contribute a lot of money and land' – and a proposal to infill part of the shore by the mouth of the river Inver to create an area for housing. 'It would have altered the whole flow of the Inver and would have made it very handy for dropping nets over the garden fence. I didn't think it was a very good idea.'

Edmund Vestey's mother was from Broughty Ferry outside Dundee and his father spent many holidays in Scotland. These included visits – in the early days of the twentieth century – with the headmaster of his prep school to the island of Oldany, where the schoolboy would 'help with the dogs'. His father began the family interest with the purchase of Glecanisp in 1935. 'Over the years it has gradually changed, we have added a bit, sold a bit, to try to get it into the most sensible management shape. What I have tried to do is put all the marvellous high country, to try to get, where we could, the principal natural movement of deer, under one management.

'In order to do that, we have sold some of the lower ground in order to pay for more of the high ground. We sold North Lochinver, a bit of Ledmore, a bit of Ben More Assynt, Drumrunie, Inchnadamph.'

(At 11 a.m., in what I imagine is a daily marking of that hour, Vestey's secretary, Penelope Whistler, appears, without a word, and leaves a coffee on his antique desk.)

The landowner is pleased that sheep are no longer a burden on the estate finances or the ground. At one point he employed seven shepherds, who could only manage lambing percentages of 30–60. It is impossible to make money from sheep, he observes, if you are paying someone else to look after them. 'Having taken them off, I am not sure we had appreciated how much effect they were having on the environmental side, on the growth of the heather. These things so often become apparent when you stop doing it.

'Last year we were going up the side of Loch Assynt and there was the most amazing display of wild flowers which we had never seen there before. We counted 50 varieties in the space of 200 yards. I am sure we hadn't seen them before because they had been chewed off.'

He remains unconvinced, however, that there are too many red deer on the land. 'When the RDC [Red Deer Commission] was formed, they told us we had to shoot ten per cent every year. Our keepers threw up their hands in horror and said that was suicide. We had been shooting six per cent. We have continued to shoot six per cent.

'We have found that the hinds have been going up a bit, and so we have increased the culling. We are now wondering whether we have overdone that. We have been counting them now for 15 years or more. Overall, the figure remains surprisingly constant.'

The idea of forest regeneration is just about meaningless on the entire 100,000 acres, which has next to no native woodland surviving. There are odd remnants of birch, hazel, rowan and holly, even an occasional Scots pine, but bringing back the forest with the available seed sources would be something akin to trying to fill a fridge with a single egg.

There are around one dozen areas fenced to allow the expansion of birchwoods and there is one area which has been fenced against deer for 30 years, as part of an arrangement with the old Nature Conservancy Council. 'There are some things [trees] of about six foot in it,' says Vestey. There is no rampant regeneration.

But while he disputes the fact that there are too many deer, he agrees there are too few fish. Salmon and sea trout catches have been declining for years, although the fishing still 'goes some way towards paying for itself'.

Vestey remembers that the Kirkaig was famed for its big fish, and that not a season would pass without one 25-pounder. The biggest – caught 25 years ago – was over 39lb, and would put to shame most fish caught on the much bigger Tay or the Tweed today.

'I suspect it is a combination of a lot of things, such as the netting off Greenland, and fish farms are undoubtedly having some effect; every bay has its cage. Sea trout are very, very few now, and they used to be common. The indications are very much that that is a result of the fish farms.' And he throws in his own observation of a scientific oddity in the rivers – the catching of grilse (salmon which have been to sea for one winter) weighing no more than 2lb. 'There isn't such a thing, but we are catching them.'

Vestey recalls that he read about the inheritance tax avoidance deal in *The Daily Telegraph*. 'It was something the Labour government brought in under Mr Healey as Chancellor. That places of outstanding natural beauty should be free of inheritance tax in the same way as pictures of national importance. Provided the Countryside Commission for Scotland recommended to the Exchequer that they were of outstanding natural beauty, and provided a management agreement was entered into.

'It is a very sensible, broad, commonsense arrangement. We tell them what we have done, they come to look from time to time. They are very satisfied with the way we are looking after the place.'

Those who holiday in the area and many of those who live in the area – in other words, the public who are meant to benefit from this arrangement, and who, ultimately, are paying for it – know nothing about the arrangement. Its public benefits are not explained to the public.

The sporting estate remains for Vestey – he says this without any obvious lifting of the spirits or gleam in the eye – an escape. 'Most of my holidays I used to spend up there. That indicates one has a certain attachment to the place and a certain love of the place.'

But the love may not extend to the local community. He recalls the occasion when the Highlands and Islands Development Board wanted to extend Lochinver harbour to cope with a new interest in fishing. 'They said Lochinver couldn't be without a hotel, so I built another one. Then they didn't knock down the old one [Willie Hutchison's Culag].' The old one, he adds with a sense of ownership, which his father had rebuilt in the 1930s following a fire.

He continues, without prompting, to say that he has not been in the Culag Hotel since the day he sold it. But he recalls that one couple moved up the hill to his Inverlodge Hotel after one night on the harbour. 'It may be there is a demand for the cheaper, rougher accommodation, but we have tried to put in an up-market, good, comfortable hotel of a high standard.' It is the kind of comment that is readily chewed over, and regurgitated, by the local community.

(Author's travel note: The Culag is a reasonably priced hotel, with recent décor and, by Highland standards, good food. However, I was not able to compare it with the new hotel on the hill.)

The original estate house, Glencanisp Lodge, is 'a fair size', according to Vestey, and his wife suggested, after 25 years as visiting housekeeper, that enough was enough. 'We have built a much smaller one, much easier to run, much less for my wife to worry about. And it is nice and handy for the new hotel.'

He has been asked frequently in recent years to give his views on the new neighbouring landowner – the Crofters' Trust. 'It is an interesting experiment. I am not sure they have anything they hadn't got already, apart from being able to say they own the land. They had the grazing rights, and the ability to buy their own croft. They are able to say they are proud owners, but it has cost them quite a lot of money to achieve that. They had everything except the title to the land.'

I have the feeling that somewhere along the past six decades the relationship between laird and community has deteriorated to such an extent that it is irreparable. His conversation – unlike that of Paul van Vlissengen, owner of Letterewe estate – only turns to community matters when it is to point out that he has resisted a bad idea or is unimpressed with the look of something in the neighbourhood.

And there is no commitment to preserving community life implicit in his own brief summation of his responsibilities as an owner: 'In my opinion it doesn't matter who the owner is, or where he comes from, or whatever, as long as he appreciates what it is he owns and respects it and does his best to pass it on to whoever comes next in good credit. That is the only thing that matters.'

As I head off into unconvincing sleet, I am left with the impression that 'whoever comes next' is the next Vestey, and not the offspring of the council tenants in Baddidarach.

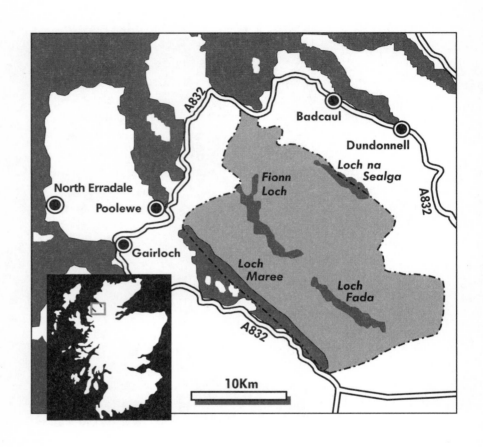

ACREAGE – 87,000
OWNER – PAUL VAN VLISSINGEN, DUTCH BUSINESSMAN
MANAGED FOR – CONSERVATION, SPORT, THE SPIRIT
POINTS OF INTEREST – LARGEST ESTATE OWNED BY A
FOREIGNER

CHAPTER TWO

Letterewe Estate

P eter the chauffeur is standing by the baggage reclaim point in Terminal 1, holding a sign which says Conholt Park. He is waiting to take me to Paul van Vlissingen's permanent residence, a country mansion sitting high above a valley on the chalky border of Hampshire and Wiltshire. The square house at the end of a tree-lined drive is set in soft countryside, a far cry and several hundred miles from the northern outpost of van Vlissingen's world, the spectacular Letterewe Estate in Wester Ross.

In 1994, conscious of the fact that he was spending more than his allotted 90 days a year in the UK, the urbane Dutchman made England his main home. Yet the dramatic corner of Scotland that is Letterewe remains a passion, an obsessive love which he indulges on a regular basis.

The two estates were chosen for the quality of their landscape by a man who is as much interested in nourishing the spirit, as the bank balance. As one of Europe's richer men, it is an idiosyncrasy he can afford.

He admits to falling in love with land and scenery, to feeling something that is 'far greater than me' in the areas he owns. He talks about guardianship, rather than ownership, styling himself as someone who will take decisions which reflect the aesthetic considerations of property, as much as the day-to-day practicalities. He wanted to pass on the land no worse than he found it. Landscape is put before commerce. Mining companies are turned down in favour of the local shepherd.

At Letterewe, his great interest is the herd of red deer, descendants of the same animals which were studied in detail by the naturalist Frank Fraser Darling in 1937. He has endeavoured to improve the vitality and strength of the animals in his 17 years of ownership; he and his friends and his stalkers shoot only the poorer, weaker animals.

At Conholt, he is trying to create the perfect pheasant shoot for his guests. He wants the birds to slip and slide from the guns, to have more than a sporting chance of escape. And he waxes eloquent about the hunter's instinct – a force which he believes is latent in most of us. Time and again, he says, he has seen young people, often women, say they could never shoot a deer and then become involved in stalking and give in to the old instinct: the hunting genes.

He is an inveterate supporter of hunting, but a lover of nature, a keen photographer of the natural world – usually in close-up – occasionally a writer, a reader of poetry and an amateur philosopher. His partner, Caroline Tisdall, former Guardian correspondent and a director of the Countryside Alliance, writes poetry to accompany his photography. Like many Dutchmen, he is a professor of compromise; he is appalled by the confrontational politics of Westminster, and he inhabits a world in which dialogue with the opposition is the only route towards success.

His views on the inherited problems of the Highland environment may need polishing, but Paul van Vlissingen is a rare breath of fresh air in the stuffy world of Scottish land-ownership. He espouses a new period of co-operation with communities, recreation and environment groups, displaying a commonsense attitude which appears alien to more reactionary lairds.

He is chairman of one of the biggest privately owned trading companies in the world, the hugely successful – not a single loss in 200 years – SHV, a food and energy group which employs 65,000 people in 25 countries, and includes household names such as Calor Gas and Makro superstores.

The M4 is awash with water and cars. It is a soaking day in early January and Peter the cockney chauffeur is taking it easy. You do not have to be part of Paul van Vlissingen's world to be aware of the wealth and privilege which surround him. It is enough to be *en route* to one of his homes. Travel to Letterewe lodge in Wester Ross and you have to leave the real world behind at the pierside on Loch Maree while his launch or his cattle float ferries you over the deep waters to the roadless north shore.

On the way to Conholt, it is Peter's chat which denotes the otherworldliness of this businessman's environment.

His routine tasks, he tells me, include driving the Scottish deerhounds, the Labrador and the Bavarian mountain stag hound from Conholt to Letterewe for the boss's sojourns in the north. His first trip with the dogs was his first visit to Scotland, and to one of the most beautiful parts of the country. He uses a Range Rover for these journeys but today he is driving a 'continuous four-wheel drive, a very rare model' BMW estate car, 'with 16-inch wheels'. His Dutch police driving instructor taught him to drive with his hands in the classic ten to two position, a position, we agree, which no one ever uses for long journeys.

As we enter the drive at Conholt, Peter pulls over and hops out to put on his jacket. 'I have to look the part,' he confides, 'but it is not very comfortable to drive in.' Van Vlissingen is at the door with Caroline Tisdall, Tuesday and Wednesday the striking deer-hounds, Monday the black Labrador and Saturday the Bavarian deer-hound, which looks like, and is nicknamed, Piglet.

The Dutchman is tall, handsome and a youthful 50-something. He is in woolly jumper and cords. Mrs T (as she is known at Letterewe) is in a trouser suit of the local MacKenzie tartan. A log fire is blazing in the white marble fireplace, the regulation country house draught is swirling above the polished floorboards, and fresh coffee is served.

When Letterewe estate — more accurately Kernsary, Ardlair and Fisherfield — was put on the market by the brewer Bill Whitbread in

1977, Paul van Vlissingen had been on the lookout for a Scottish property for some time. He had fond memories of trips to the Highlands with his mother, when he was a boy in the late 1940s, and as a student he began to nurture the idea of having more regular contact with the place. At an early age he was moved by the grandeur and openness of some of the oldest mountains in the world. Hardly surprising, perhaps, for a native of Holland.

He was telephoned by a friend in Scotland to be told that he would have to move fast to secure the Wester Ross estate, a 'unique opportunity'. He chose a characteristically odd route to ownership.

'Did I tell you about how I bought Letterewe? I got on a flight and rented a car. I decided the best thing was not to walk in Letterewe but to drive around it, and look at it with 'binos', driving around all the pubs, offering free drinks to everybody in the pubs from Kinlochewe to Gairloch and Poolewe and round to Dundonnel. I decided to talk to the locals, and by the end I had a pretty good picture.

'They said it was a wild place. A place with a long history. I got a very good feeling about what the locals also thought was their land. I presented myself as a tourist who was interested in the area. When I finished the last pub, I said I would buy it. On the recommendation of the locals. I bought it without ever seeing the place.'

He paid around £500,000 for the original 48,000 acres, another £400,000 for a later 12,000, and £1.5 million for the Little Gruinard river and surrounding area in 1989. He has since added north Kinlochewe (including Slioch) to his land, and restored the estate to its original, geographically sensible, boundaries.

What he had seen, during his pub investigation, was a good enough indicator of what makes the place so special. Letterewe is an almost roadless, wild place bounded by Loch Maree on the south, and Loch na Sealga on the north. It is a fastness of spectacular mountains, including An Teallach, the anvil, and Slioch, the spear. It contains over 20 lochs, including formidable Fionn Loch, the deceptively named White Loch, a six-mile sweep of mountain water, stretching from the head of the little Gruinard salmon river to a natural amphitheatre of mountains which includes Am Maidchen, the Maiden, one of the remotest Munros in Britain. Fionn can be a still, beautiful place, despite the loss of its surrounding pine and birch forests, and it can be transformed in minutes by westerly winds sweeping unobstructed from the Atlantic which make it a place of steep waves and swirling spindrift.

You can see none of this detail from the road from Kinlochewe along the south side of Loch Maree. But you can see the essence of it; the ramparts of ancient gneiss mountains rising above Loch Maree; glimpses of the far, brown interior. It was never a real crofting estate, never a place which was well peopled.

'I remember standing by a farm where you could look away to the right towards the estate. It was one of those still days, there was snow on the mountains, and I remember the enormous scale of the landscape, the nearly touchable silence.

'You cannot explain it in rational, scientific terms, but it was far more important than how many stags had been shot. They all said there were hundreds of deer. They did not see it as something romantic.

'My first impression when I went to the place was the absolutely timeless beauty of it. There is something that is so far beyond the little human heartbeat. It gave me the feeling that I was buying something that was much bigger than I was myself – in terms of value, or philosophy.'

His feeling for the place hasn't changed much since. With his partner, he as created as good a relationship with the locals as an essentially absent owner could hope to achieve. 'There is a deep-rooted anti-English feeling, more than an anti-foreigner feeling. The Dutch and the Scottish have always traded. I don't think we have ever felt any antagonistic feeling in the area.'

He is defensive of foreign ownership of Scottish lands – a huge area of Wester Ross is now in Dutch hands – on the basis that the world is not going the way of narrow nationalism. 'The world is going in a devolutionary way. I would always feel a sympathy for a Scottish Parliament, I come from a very small country. I can see the millions of problems and the fact that it would not solve very much, but I can see the feeling of wanting to belong to a smaller entity.' But why should Scotland become any more restrictive than China, India or

Chile? His idea of devolution is encompassed within an all-embracing global economy which has few effective boundaries, a world which he understands, and a world somewhat larger than the Scottish National Party's 'Europe of regions'.

Van Vlissingen has a sense of fairness which affects his dealings with the community, an attitude in which might be seen echoes of the lost paternalism of the early eighteenth-century clan chieftains. When he decided he would like a small swimming-pool at his whitewashed lodge on the north shore of Loch Maree, he felt the equivalent facility should be available to the villagers. 'I was horrified to learn that many of the local children could not swim. This was amazing for somebody coming from Holland.' He offered £20,000 to the local community towards a swimming-pool fund, and the locals did the rest. They held fairs, concerts, a plastic-duck race on the river Ewe, and trebled the amount of money he had provided. The swimming-pool now exists and is 'washing its face'.

Another story, of a tragic accident, confirms the owner's relationship with the local people. In the 1980s a remote stalker's bothy at Larachantivore on the north side of the estate burst into flames following a petrol leak. Two young ghillies, one 21 the other 31, died in the blaze.

After the funeral of the younger victim, the only son of a couple in Poolewe, the bereaved parents placed an advertisement in the local paper, thanking Paul van Vlissingen and Caroline Tisdall for their help after the tragedy. The wife of the second victim, who was from Aberdeen, read out at his funeral the diary which he had kept at the bothy and which spoke of his awe for a dramatic landscape.

Van Vlissingen has since fenced off a small area at the site of the bothy and planted the same number of trees as the combined ages of the two men. Caroline Tisdall wrote a poem, which is there on a plaque. The owner writes to the families every autumn, on the anniversary of the accident, to tell them how the plantation is doing.

There is no doubt that the appreciation of the spiritual element of such wild places, as expressed by the ghillie, is one that is familiar to the laird, and probably to many landowners. It is a feeling that may not be expressed in the same way by the locals who live and work in the Highlands, although they may appreciate what they have during the odd visit to London or some other city. It is an appreciation, of the type promoted by the Wilderness Trust which reintroduces people to nature, of the spiritual value of communion with wilderness.

The Highlands are far from being wilderness, but they are undoubtedly wild, particularly in areas such as the heart of Letterewe, where there are no ghosts of a crofting community cleared to the coastal margin, or clean away to Canada. Van Vlissingen does not have to deal with historical guilt. But then it is doubtful if he would view it that way.

He says the influence of one individual on the landscape should not be over-emphasised, that one person can do little to affect or damage his surroundings. And yet he goes on to claim, rightly, that he has had a pretty significant influence on Letterewe in terms of preserving it as he found it.

He loses around £100,000 a year running the estate, and does not grudge it. 'Once you go north-west of Inverness, every estate costs money. You might break even south-east of Inverness if you have grouse and sheep subsidies and timber and fishing from the Spey or the Tweed. I would be very surprised if, north-west of Loch Ness, there was a single estate that makes a profit.

'That means that it is not necessarily financial criteria which come into play, but criteria of a certain single-mindedness. The same single-mindedness where people want to have an extraordinary building, or an extraordinary picture, or to protect the tigers in India. I am buying that, because of its conservation qualities. I never bought Letterewe with any idea that I would make one penny out of it. It is costing me a lot of money. But I have never had one second of regret. I have this wonderful feeling that I contribute to society in a way that gives me great pleasure, but gives other people pleasure as well.

'I think the most important responsibility of a so-called landowner in Scotland with a large chunk of land is to protect it against fashions, against short-term issues and to give it time. If I stopped my deer management policy the deer would degenerate somewhat, but that wouldn't be very serious in terms of landscape.'

Several years ago he was approached by a mining company which wanted to look for minerals by drilling test bores. It offered, in return, to create a road from the stalker's house at Kernsary all the way to the remote bothy and house at Carnmore in the centre of the mountain estate. Carnmore is a place which has to be reached at present by a long walk, or by a four-mile boat trip along Fionn Loch; it is a place beloved of climbers, and the innumerable German backpackers who have a knack of finding the best bits of other people's countries.

Van Vlissingen turned down the mining company. He turned down the proposal for a hydro-electric scheme at the west end of Fionn. And he remains opposed to putting new tracks into his estate. He has made an exception for one proposed track – which has since been passed by a public inquiry – alongside the Little Gruinard, because he believes it will benefit the last shepherd working on the estate.

However, perhaps his single greatest contribution to land-owning in Scotland has been his involvement in the access debate with ramblers and mountaineers. After two years of round-table talks at Letterewe – precipitated by the owner as his response to carping criticism of his access policy – the parties involved agreed the Letterewe Accord, a blueprint for access to private land which was co-written by Caroline Tisdall and Dave Morris of the Ramblers Association.

It states that access is based on the principle of the freedom to roam, and it as been adopted by neighbouring (mainly Dutch) estates in Wester Ross. Van Vlissingen, largely through the encouragement of his partner, solved the access problem on his land without any need for legislative measures that guarantee a 'right of responsible access' to the countryside. If the same attitude had been adopted on other estates, there would have been less confrontation over the years and less need for a new law to force lairds to accept walkers in the hills. Yet van Vlissingen did not receive telephone calls from other owners, or their factors, asking him how on earth he had managed to protect his stalking. The answer, in fact, was simple. Talk.

The agreement at Letterewe, hailed as a major breakthrough by the access groups, still asks walkers to contact the estate between 15 September and 15 November, and those people who do so may well be asked to walk elsewhere or avoid a certain area. That is all the protection which most sporting estates want, and yet they often fail to end up on the right side of the voluntary groups because of a mutual distrust.

'Foreigners can bring in a very welcome new way of thinking,' remarks the Dutchman. 'I wouldn't say foreign ownership is negative at all. The most Victorian and reactionary landowner I know is Scottish.

'I am a practical man when I want to achieve something. I see for the future of the estates that the allies of the estate owner are the bodies who represent the outdoor interest. The estate owner doesn't have any friends or allies in politics just by owning land [many Scots would dispute this remark!], and there is an excellent chance for compromise on all sorts of issues between environmentalists and mountaineers and estate owners. Society exists because it is based on common sense, middle groups, and not on the extremes. If it is based on the extremes, you get the Hitlers.'

He is a champion of private land-ownership, partly because of what he has seen in the Eastern European countries where state ownership was the norm, and has left today a legacy of appalling pollution and environmental degradation, and partly because he simply believes it is one of the best options.

'Probably land-ownership in all countries should be a chequered board, with something owned by landowners, by nature groups, by small farmers, large farmers, by the state.' He dismisses the suggestion that private ownership on a large scale is unpopular with the Scottish public at large. 'If the Scottish people wanted to buy estates, it would cost peanuts. If there was a movement of millions of Scots who wanted it to happen, then it could happen.' 'Maybe it will happen,' adds Caroline.

'The fact that these estates come up for sale so frequently, it would probably only take one generation to own half of all the big estates in Scotland.'

He is equally dismissive of the common criticisms of absentee landowners – that they are too remote to have a useful influence on the land, that they are out of touch with what is happening in

Scotland. He maintains that absentee ownership is not a problem for Letterewe and the surrounding community.

'The use of the word "absentee" gives the suggestion that it is a landlord who is not interested. I would be very much against that. That landlord has not fallen in love with the land.

'However, you may be working very hard at business life in Edinburgh or Berlin while a lot of your thoughts are going into the land. I don't think physical presence would be my yardstick.' He keeps in touch on a regular basis by fax and phone, and employs the same form of 'pancake management' in land-owning which he employs in his successful business: there are direct lines of communication between senior managers and those at the coal face. He tries, as far as possible, to cut out intermediaries, which means that while he is in China working on the opening of a new chain of Makro stores, he remains in contact – mainly by fax – with Barbara Grant, wife of head stalker Graeme Grant, at Letterewe lodge.

And here is the heart of his estate management philosophy. 'I am very well known for not liking factors. Factors are, historically, and quite often in practice, out of date. They have a sell-by date which was yesterday. The way the world is, is for direct contact between people, and not for intermediaries. You want to have a direct connection with your employees.

'You can always call in experts if you need them, scientific experts for example. The factor will ask the lawyer or another expert for the same advice in the same way, and give the impression on the estate that the boss is beyond direct contact. That is wrong in management.'

Contact with the estate, however, and regular visits to the land, do not guarantee that an owner can remain well informed on the latest debates. Van Vlissingen sees the key role of the landowner in simple terms – remember, for example, his suggestion that the role of the owner is to protect the land against fashions.

At the core of current environmental concern and thinking in Scotland is the role of the forest, and the loss of the forest culture which once thrived in Scotland in the way that it survives today in Scandinavia. Put simply, many people want to expand the surviving 1 to 2 per cent of native woodland – pine, birch, oak, hazel, rowan, aspen and co – and by so doing, restore some of the fertility and productivity which has been lost from Scottish soil and water over many hundreds of years. At the same time, woodland (ideally, owned by the local community) would be a source of fuel, timber, fruit, wildlife, tourist revenue and – to be romantic about it – spiritual uplift.

Very few of those arguing for regeneration and planting schemes – now supported by woodland grants from the Forestry Authority – see trees as a single issue, in isolation from the wider habitat and the wildlife that depends on it. Like the red deer, for example, which are the heart of the sporting estate management in the Highlands.

The considerable achievements of the Royal Society for the Protection of Birds at its Abernethy estate in the Cairngorms is a prime example of what is possible. The Caledonian pine forest is regenerating there, without the use of deer fencing, because the deer numbers have been reduced to a level at which the animals do not destroy all the young seedlings on the ground. The result is the creation of a stunningly beautiful woodland landscape, of thick heather, bursting juniper and blaeberries, of young pine and birch, of plump capercaillies – and of red deer and roe deer.

Van Vlissingen, although he has birch regeneration schemes on the Little Gruinard, has a very black-and-white view of the trees debate. 'Environmentalists generally are always part of a fashion. The debate is far too short to see whether they are talking nonsense or not. There is little scientific evidence. I asked the scientists whether they could tell me whether any studies had been done on the population dynamics of red deer in Scotland. Nobody knows why there are more deer.

'I think environmentalists have jumped on the bandwagon out of fashion, and suddenly you will have to have Scottish pine everywhere. I would rather do some practical research.

'I would not dispute that it [reforestation] could actually be done. I do take issue with the fact that it is anything but a human choice. I do not believe in the so-called scientific valuation that a forest has a higher biological value than the moor.' He mentions the insectivorous plant sundew (which should be celebrated in this country for its midge-eating properties), which is rare and protected in Holland, suggesting that it may be every bit as important as the more charismatic mammals of the pine forest.

'Until now, the debate by the tree people has been very one sided, emotional and unscientific. They talk about the management of landscape. If you like to look at moor, you manage the moor, if you happen to like trees, you manage trees. My objection to the debate is that all the deer in Scotland have to be shot to allow the trees to grow.' In this last statement he appears, for the first time, closer to the prevailing views of the more reactionary landowners who distrust the environmental interest in Highland Scotland.

On Letterewe estate, like most other Highland estates, there has been little regeneration in recent years due to the pressure of grazing animals, principally deer and wild goats. Van Vlissingen believes there is no over-population of red deer because the numbers are roughly what they were when Frank Fraser Darling was studying the animals in the 1930s, from his cottage at Dundonnel on the northern reaches of the land. Fraser Darling, however, was studying the behaviour of the animals, and not their impact on the land. He would almost certainly have thought there were too many.

It is quite common for landowners in the west to point out that there are the same number of animals on the land today as there have been for generations, therefore there is no over-population. Yet the proof is patently obvious. Where there is no regeneration of woodland, the numbers of gazing animals, whether deer, or goat or sheep, or rabbits, or all four, are – objectively, at least – too high.

However, to prove that he is prepared to listen, van Vlissingen has undertaken a number of woodland projects and, since reading the first edition of this book, has fenced a large area around the Beannach Mor and Beannoch Beag lochs on the south side of Fionn. He is waiting to see if regeneration can occur on impoverished spoil, with few seed sources. The move is highly laudable, although the kick-start of planting may prove to be necessary.

Yet in the centre of Fionn there are islands which have been declared Sites of Special Scientific Interest because of their bursting life. Because they are not grazed by all but the most adventurous of deer, they are covered in trees, shrubs and berry-bearing plants. On a still summer's day these islands are places of enchanting beauty, haunted by the trickling song of the warbler and the rustle of the Atlantic breeze in birch leaves. A few hundred years ago the same islands were used as nest sites by the ospreys and the sea eagles which were persecuted to extinction, partly by the former owner – the family of Osgood MacKenzie, creator of Inverewe Gardens. MacKenzie himself, in his book *One Hundred Years of the Highlands and Islands*, records a remarkable litany of destruction, glorifying his own teenage exploits with the rifle and revelling in the taking of the last sea eagle's egg from Fionn. And then wondering, as if two and two never made four, why sea eagles had disappeared from the area.

These islands are like the areas of the Highlands where crofting is still carried on according to the best environment and community-friendly traditions, and where the sight of a genuine crofting township can be uplifting in a sparse landscape. I do not find it possible to visit these islands – or their much larger equivalent on Loch Maree – without finding the surrounding moorland imperfect. People, landowners among them, have been too quick to accept the bare Highland hills, which are no more natural than a cleared crofting township.

Down on the edge of Loch Maree, where the remains of the old charcoal kilns can still be found in the surviving oakwoods, there is one area not far from Letterewe lodge which has been deer-fenced for around 20 years. According to Dick Balharry of Scottish Natural Heritage, the regeneration in that area is 'fantastic', showing a natural progression of birch and rowan. But Vlissingen remarks that the young oaks are missing. The reason may simply be that young oak need open areas in the canopy to thrive, and that they might do best on the edge of existing wood. On the edge of this wood, all the tasty young plants are grazed by a large population of wild goats, and by deer.

Van Vlissengen agrees that deer would do better, and grow larger, in woodland cover. But he is fascinated by progression. 'Species mutate through thousands of years. The mutation of the deer in Scottish hills has been an adaptation of the fact that there was no cover or forestry. If you compare them with the deer I used to shoot in Austria, there the deer weigh twice as much. It is a totally different environment, totally different, but I would find it hard to say that one was better than the other.

'I am interested in deer as a biological phenomenon. In this place [Conholt] we have a ten-year programme of tree planting, specimen trees, regeneration of woods, but I don't like the argument of putting one against the other.

'The deerstalking for me is secondary. I like and admire the wild creature that survives all that weather, all those storms, all that snow and survives in that very difficult landscape. But if you took the debate to the extreme, if there were no trees in Scotland, I would be one of the first to say you should do something about that.'

From the point of view of SNH, the RSPB, the World Wide Fund for Nature, Reforesting Scotland, Natural Resources Scotland, and a host of others, there are next to no trees in Scotland, and forests represent a major biological and economic opportunity.

Meantime, following his innovative work on access, van Vlissingen has launched a three-year project aimed at studying the biology of the deer and the botany of the estate. The results should allow Letterewe to implement sustainable strategies for deer management. Respected scientists are overseeing the work, and the findings could have a wider impact on how deer are managed on Scottish sporting estates. The initiative was prompted in part by the Deer Commission, which demanded, without scientific justification, that the hind cull should be trebled. Van Vlissingen rejects its figures as crude and generalised. The Deer Commission cannot afford to study every single estate in detail, and so applies general principles to its demands in a bid to drastically reduce the number of hinds throughout the Highlands. The owner would like to do things differently.

Van Vlissingen uses the estate for his own personal relaxation and he encourages friends and family to visit. Business associates have found the place a positive incentive to deal-making. And the owner has always involved the four stalkers very much in the day-to-day running of the property.

A number of commentators have remarked that if Scotland must have absentee landowners, then they ought to be like Paul van Vlissingen. His contribution to the access debate has been important, as have his talks to land-owning audiences. When he addressed an audience of owners and land agents at Battleby outside Perth a few years ago, he delivered a useful message – on the importance and the power of dialogue and compromise, the importance of listening to logic outside your own experience. Rare enough characteristics in Scottish politics, land-owning, agencies and local authorities.

Van Vlissingen may yet walk in Abernethy, or on the Creag Meagaidh National Nature Reserve, and accept that there is sound justification for some restoration of land which is well below its biological potential. His approach to ownership, coupled with the wealth which allows him to lose money and to turn down economic opportunity, make possible a fantastic demonstration on Letterewe estate of a future landscape for the West Highlands, in which the open hill and deerstalking could remain very much part of a better whole.

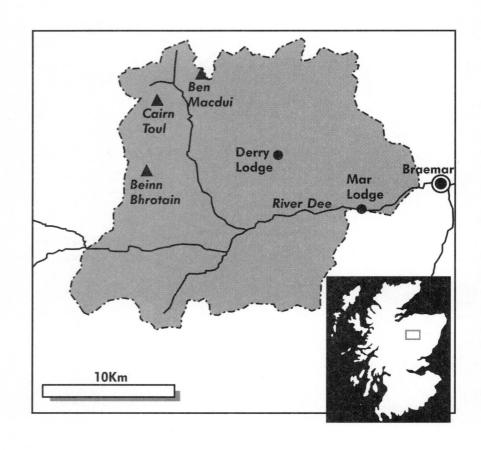

ACREAGE – 77,500
OWNER – NATIONAL TRUST FOR SCOTLAND
MANAGED FOR – CONSERVATION AND SPORT
POINTS OF INTEREST – BOUGHT FOR A BELLY-DANCER, NOW
'SAVED FOR THE NATION'

CHAPTER THREE

Mar Lodge Estate

Even on a dreich July day the remnants of the Caledonian pine forest are hung with mist and magic. Trees two centuries old stand in small groups, appearing black in silhouette on cloudy horizons. Under cover of the old canopy, even in the dullest weather, the needles are a vivid green and hung with a million drips. On the forest floor, thousands of wood ants tramp roads between heather and juniper, climbing anthills more than three feet high, hauling twigs four times their length. The ants are threatened by the loss of native pinewood.

At the edge of Lui Water, 150 stags, their new antlers still covered in velvet, graze the wet grass. In Gaelic they are sometimes called the 'children of the mist' and for the passing walkers and mountain bikers, making a steady and colourful trickle towards the heart of the Cairngorms and the Lairig Ghru pass, they help to make the day. Few of those who pass will realise that the stirring sight of these stags, the biggest land mammals left in the UK, are a solid illustration of the crisis facing the ecology of Mar Lodge estate. Ironically, they were, until recently, also viewed as its wealth. Private estates are valued and sold to successive owners according to the size of the sporting bag. The real health of the land, and its conservation value, has little to do with the transactions.

It is a long leap, you might think, from the Danish Sex Fair and a rather uncelebrated film called *The Nine Stages of Nakedness* to ownership of a hugely important Scottish estate. But you would be wrong.

For Patricia Kluge, formerly the wife of soft-porn publisher Russell Gay, it was a move accomplished with ease. Within a decade of appearing full-frontal in husband number one's publication, *Knave*, she had made the transition to *Town & Country*, fully clothed. Husband number two, as well as being 34 years older and five inches shorter, happened to be the ninth richest man in the world, the second richest in America.

When Patricia married John Kluge in New York in 1981, the odd couple set about wooing high society on both sides of the Atlantic. She appeared alongside Ivana Trump and Johnny Carson in the USA, and wanted to do the equivalent in Britain: the belly-dancer wanted to meet the royal family.

With money, such things are made easier. The formerly retiring Kluge bought a London mansion not far from Buckingham Palace, followed by Mar Lodge estate in the Cairngorms. The Highland estate was visited by Patricia while she was on holiday in Scotland and was bought unseen by her husband for just under £7 million. It was one more wedding gift. Mar Lodge is just 12 miles from Balmoral Castle.

The couple almost certainly did not know that it was also part of one of the most important tracts of wild land in Scotland, and an area in urgent need of sympathetic conservation management.

The Kluges cultivated (invested money in) the exclusive sports of polo and carriage-driving – one, the favourite of the Prince of Wales, the other, the passion of Prince Philip. Patricia got to know both men but failed in her attempts to meet the Queen. The real reason for this is not known but there is some tantalising speculation. There is every chance it had more to do with the outlandish tales from the couple's Virginian estate, Albemarle, than with Patricia's history in a G-string.

The young millionairess arranged pheasant shoots on the USA's blue-grass country. According to American press reports, they were more like pheasant slaughters, with as many as 600 birds shot in a single day. Shooting pheasants is one thing, killing the neighbourhood dogs and every other potential predator, another.

In November 1988 – a few months before the purchase of Mar

Lodge – seven hawk carcasses were found tied to a string. A few days later an anonymous letter led to a police investigation. In one of the estate waste pits, officers found the rotting bodies of more than 300 protected birds, many foxes and a dozen dogs, including a beagle full of lead shot which was still wearing a collar inscribed with the name of its owner, a local policeman. A shocked Patricia declared she and her husband knew nothing of the massacre. 'We came to the country to devote our lives to the accumulation of historic farms, to preserve and protect . . . nature . . . and its species.' In this, she was no different from the Scottish landowner who claims no knowledge of the poisoned golden eagle found on the grouse moor.

The English sporting manager of the estate, Sir Richard Musgrave, and the gamekeepers, Paul Shardlow and David Amos, were arrested and later convicted in the US District Court in Charlottesville. They were fined $12,500 each and given suspended jail sentences. Shortly after the trial they left the country, their fines and their fares paid by Kluge.

But the damage was done. The Prince and Princess of Wales cancelled a planned visit to the Kluges and the tabloid press grabbed the story like a ferret scenting a rabbit. What a happy cocktail for British newsdesks – a porn star, mixed up with the killing of furry animals, who had just become the mistress of a Highland estate. PORNO QUEEN GUNS FOR EAGLES said *The Sun* headline in January 1989.

In some ways, Patricia and John Kluge had enjoyed similar life experiences, dragging themselves to material heights from humble beginnings. Kluge started out as a poor immigrant and saved every dime until the point at which Rupert Murdoch bought his television empire for $2 billion. He was born in Germany in 1914 but brought up by his mother and stepfather in America, where he was awarded a scholarship to Columbia. He studied economics and was almost expelled for gambling. To improve his income he worked three shifts in the dining-hall and ran a secretarial service from his room.

He graduated in 1937, got a job as a distributor with a food company and, by 1940, had saved enough money to buy a radio station in silver Springs, Maryland. He then set about gathering other stations and creating the giant media, food and property corporation which he still heads today, the New York and Washington-based Metromedia Inc.

Patricia, the daughter of a British businessman and a half-Scottish half-Iraqi mother, began life in some luxury in Baghdad, before finding herself with her divorced mother in a small London flat.

While Kluge was making money on one side of the Atlantic, Patricia was on the other, becoming a belly-dancer in a Bayswater pub called the Labyrinth and kicking off the Danish Sex Fair of 1970 with a striptease. She met and married porn publisher Russell Gay in 1973, wrote a 'good sex' column for his magazine, and soon went her separate way. She met Kluge at a dinner party in New York.

The purchase of Mar Lodge was hardly a financial challenge for the American. He had paid $1.5 million for a fortieth birthday party for Patricia at the Waldorf-Astoria. Guests, including Armand Hammer, Empress Farah of Iran and the Sangsters – Kluge had an interest in his racing stable – fished in a lake of caviar for ice sculptures containing bottles of Russian vodka, while two orchestras played 'Happy Birthday'. A New York socialite remarked that the event was on the scale of a great charity gala, with no charity to benefit.

When the couple separated in 1991, Kluge had no reason to retain Mar Lodge. In 1992, a conservation consortium sought, unsuccessfully, to raise £10 million to buy it.

The Kluge stewardship of the important mountain area, and the latest chapter in the ownership of the property, ended in April 1995, thanks to the Heritage Lottery Fund, which decided to invest £10.2 million of lottery profits in the purchase of the estate for the National Trust for Scotland. And for the nation.

The Trust took possession in June 1995, and will pay for Mar Lodge in instalments over 15 years. Kluge will get £5.5 million for his place in the hills, compared to the £7 million he paid to buy it from the Swiss Gerard Panchaud. Panchaud purchased it for just £100,000 in 1962.

The American, displaying some affection for the place, has retained a cottage at Claybokie, not far from the lodge.

I have been asked on several occasions if I would avoid writing about a potential estate purchase, or even a development on an estate, because 'to do so would jeopardise the whole thing'. The power of the press was so great, it was averred, that one sentence out of line could damage the intention of this or that potential purchaser.

I found it hard to sympathise with most of the requests. At a 1994 Christmas drinks party for the great and good (and rather remote and stuffy) members and friends of the National Trust for Scotland, I was taken aside by a council member. 'Was I,' he wanted to know, 'going to mention the belly-dancer again?' Because if I did, he feared the NTS might not be able to secure ownership of Mar Lodge. Mr Kluge was said to be highly sensitive about such things.

Could I possibly threaten the Trust ownership of such a place? Would I do so, just to repeat the salacious gossip about Patricia Kluge? Well, yes. I have just repeated the gossip again, insulting, no doubt, the new dawn of NTS stewardship.

I have never believed that writing about John Kluge in a British national newspaper could have any effect on the ownership of the estate, nor do I pursue this particular line for the mere fact that Patricia Kluge may have brought some welcome sex and scandal to the hills. But the story of one of the world's richest men and his wife is the perfect illustration of what goes wrong with land-ownership in Scotland, and can still go wrong.

He could have been a billionaire, and she a reformed porn star, who made the perfect couple for Mar Lodge. They could have run it in exemplary fashion. In fact, there are far worse examples of estate management in Scotland by more traditional lairds. On the plus side, Kluge appointed the odd Tudor/Victorian lodge to a standard of ludicrous luxury, regularly flying his American designer to Deeside to sort out the fine details of a place where he spent little of his valuable time. Is that a plus?

Yet he steadfastly refused to offer any public profile or to explain his policies. His ownership made a mockery of successive government claims that the mechanisms exist in this country to deliver conservation goals. It is accepted internationally – not just in the UK – that the Cairngorms National nature Reserve is of great importance. But the 17,000 acres of that reserve inside mar Lodge were owned by a man who refused to discuss his plans for the land, who spent no more than two or three weeks a year in the area, and who had next to no understanding of conservation and the importance of habitats and species. A man whose agents were instructed not to co-operate with the press.

Imagine. Could Yellowstone National Park have been bought by an absentee Arab oil tycoon, or a Swiss businessman? Would the authorities then allow such an owner to promote the over-population of one particular mammal – in this case, the red deer – in order to enjoy his sport at the expense of the natural habitat?

Mar Lodge revealed, better than anywhere else, that the system of land 'protection' in Scotland is not much better than that which exists in the rainforests of South America, where outside corporations and ranchers can buy great chunks of land and do with them what they want. There are limits, of course, to what the owner could choose to do on Mar Lodge.

He could not, for example, choose to cut down the 200-year-old pine trees on the valley floor and sides – the last natural regeneration happened around the late 1700s. But he could choose to do nothing to protect them. He could kill them by neglect and allow the seedlings they produced every year, and had done for more than 200 years, to be eaten by deer.

He could not dam the river. But he could preside over its demise as over-grazing led to heavy run-off from the hills, causing erosion and collapse of the banks and the loss of vital spawning redds used for centuries by returning salmon.

And all the fine words from neighbouring landowners – even from Scottish Natural Heritage – about Mr Kluge not doing a bad job on the estate mean next to nothing, and do absolutely nothing to take away from the fact that an area holding rare alpine/arctic flora and fauna and crucial remnants of native woodland should not be treated as a bauble.

The biggest shock of all should be the fact that the public accepted this as a legitimate way to use Scotland's natural heritage. Or, more accurately, they didn't know about Mar Lodge, and therefore didn't much care.

The estate has now become the Trust's biggest property and its greatest test. It will either make or break the group's reputation on environmental matters, and by that token it is a significant challenge for an organisation which has failed to implement conservation management on other mountain properties, including Glencoe.

At the end of 1999, and four years into NTS ownership, the signs are positive. In just four winters the deer numbers have been cut from 3,300 to 1,650 and already seedlings are beginning to get above the height at which they are normally eaten by the deer. The Trust is also removing long stretches of unsightly stalking tracks bulldozed on the Mar Lodge mountains. Undoubtedly, it has moved more quickly, and more radically, than many people expected. It has appointed Adam Watson, at one time its chief critic, as a scientific adviser. And, most pertinently, it aims to expand the old forests without the use of deer fences. Fences protect trees, but they also kill woodland birds and do not create natural woodlands.

Mar Lodge is not just important because of its pinewoods, although they get most of the attention. There should be a full range of forest ecosystems, from the river edge to the birch scrub on the high hills, and the estate is equally important for the plants and animals on the plateaux and high corries, including the snow bunting, ptarmigan and the dotterel – all of them at the southern limit of their natural range. The property ranges from the floor of the River Dee to the summit of Ben Macdui, and is home to capercaillie, the peregrine falcon and the golden eagle. It should be the habitat of the crested tit, but is not, perhaps because the pinewoods are now scattered and degraded. It was once home to the wolf and the beaver.

It contains four of the six highest peaks in Britain and a total of 14 Munros; part of the largest area of alpine soils in the country; the highest heather moor in the UK; the most extensive areas of snowbed vegetation; nationally rare communities of heather and blaeberry heath at high altitude; the best examples of arctic-alpine lochs in the country.

Then – and this is not a treasure in the same way – there is the 30-bedroomed lodge, built between 1895 and 1899, twice destroyed by fire, and most recently rebuilt by John Kluge. The whole property, all 77,500 acres, provides employment for five stalker/rangers (a new title under NTS ownership), one foreman, four maintenance men and one caretaker.

Ownership by the Trust is to be warmly welcomed in the sense that it brings another great area of the central Cairngorms into not-for-profit ownership. Mar Lodge has joined Abernethy, owned by the Royal Society for the Protection of Birds, under the heading of conservation ownership. Unfortunately, Glen Feshie, another important neighbour, remains in private hands.

The 42,000-acre Rothiemurchus estate, east of Aviemore, remains in the hands of the Grant family, as it has done for centuries. Although it has its critics, the estate does a good job of managing the land for multi-purpose objectives, including recreation and conservation. Outside the core area is the huge Invercauld property, a forestry and sporting enterprise owned by Capt. Alwyn Farquharson, whose ancestor was a friend of Victoria and Albert. It will remain a sporting estate, with many of the attendant problems, but, who knows, perhaps the enlightened vision of the NTS will ultimately have its effect.

On a snowy day in February 1995, with NTS ownership looming, I returned to the estate with Adam Watson, the white-bearded man of the hills, retired scientist and internationally recognised expert on the ecology of the Cairngorms. He has studied the history of the property and documented the Clearances of 1850, which – unlike those elsewhere in the Highlands – were carried out in order to replace the people with deer, rather than sheep. The Clearances were perpetrated by the then owner, the Earl of Fife, who had expressed concern in his diaries from 1783–92 over the scarcity of deer on his land.

The earl's family had not long had the estate at this point. They acquired it after the 1715 rising which was started by the Earl of Mar, the former Jacobite owner of what was called Mar estate, whose lands were forfeited after the failure of that venture. The feudal rights were then bought by Duff of Brace, later to become the Earl of Fife.

In the late eighteenth and early nineteenth century, the deer tended to be confined to the granite hills of Ben Macdui and the surrounding area, rather than to the more fertile ground on the valley floor and on the south side of the Dee, which was used by a large human population. The people who farmed the property grew crops in the fields and excluded, and shot, the deer.

As part of the earl's new regime, there was a crackdown on poachers and the tenants' houses were searched for guns. Within a few years, deer numbers had increased dramatically. Since then, the land has been dominated by its red deer and the consequent effects are plain to see. The only pine trees left today are in those areas which were either remote or steep, and therefore naturally guarded against grazing.

The mature trees are browsed to the height a stag can reach on its hind legs, and any broken branches have been stripped of bark and left like bleached whale bones on the forest floor.

You can look for miles and not see a single young tree above the heather. This does not seem so odd in Scotland. Indeed, it is the norm. It is only when you enter a glen where there is regeneration – or even look at the under-grazed verges of the A9 in some places – that you realise how land might begin to look with fewer grazing animals.

When you set out uphill from the road beyond the Linn of Dee, you start on heather which is cropped to a fine designer stubble. It is springy and easy to walk on and, if you look closely, you can find thousands of toe-high pine seedlings, some of them a year or two old, some perhaps 50 years old. By contrast, in the newly renovated grounds of the stalker's house, natural regeneration is returning apace, with birch and pine springing out of the grass. The small garden is a mini demonstration of latent natural wealth.

The further you walk uphill, the longer the heather becomes – in other words, exactly the reverse of a natural vegetation. The heather is cropped more closely lower down because the snow melts there first, and the deer spend more time on the low ground.

Watson took me to a great cathedral of a pine tree, a giant 'granny pine' which may just be the oldest pine tree in Scotland. It could, he believes, be 500 or 600 years old, and might have been a sapling at the time of Bannockburn.

Today it is a healthy, seed-bearing giant, with an enormous canopy and a tangle of limbs as thick as 200-year-old pines spreading from its huge midriff. It is a singularly magnificent reminder of what trees can be in a mature forest. Yet none of the millions of seedlings it has produced in the last 200 years has survived. Not one. There is no tree near it which is younger than 200 years.

It is now destined, at last, to see some new growth. The estate – before the NTS sale – fenced off an area including the old tree as part of a woodland grant scheme funded by the Forestry Commission. Sadly, even this potentially positive development appeared to make little sense in the form in which it was planned. The ground was to be scarified under the surviving pines to encourage regeneration and, further along the road, thousands of hardwood trees were planted and protected by the ubiquitous plastic tubes, in the assumption that the natural broad-leaved components of Caledonian pine forest, the birch and rowan and aspen and willow, were missing.

There was no need for any of this. Natural regeneration would take place without planting or scarifying. It would take place even better, even more naturally, if deer were part of the equation. Deer should be able to eat young pine trees, and be able to break the ground with their hooves, creating bare soil for young seeds to colonise. But at the time of the fencing there was no intention of reducing the deer numbers to a level at which this could take place naturally. So the animals had to be excluded.

An hour later we crossed the bridge over the Lui Water, on the road to Derry Lodge and towards the Lairig Ghru, to walk back towards the Linn of Dee. There were more than 200 stags on our right, lying down and well sheltered from the stiff westerly wind and blowing snow. Up the glen were several ugly plantations – over 1,000 acres in total – planted in the past 30 years by the Swiss who sold the land to Kluge.

If you visit the estate with a map in your hands, then the Gaelic names provide a clue, not only to the former extent of Gaeldom and the spread of old Dalriada, but to the former character of the glen. There is a rocky island in the Lui which in Gaelic is 'bird cherry island'. There is no bird cherry anywhere on Mar Lodge. One of the treeless glens is called pinewood glen, and the Gaelic word for broom crops up in several places where there is no broom. Names which, if they were in English, would be usefully inappropriate and poignant.

On the road back to Braemar, just opposite the lodge, around 150 hinds were running along the riverside, heading towards open ground. On the edge of the village itself, hinds could be seen grazing in the damaged birchwood where the barely surviving juniper was no more than a foot high, in scattered clumps.

The farm to the east of the lodge was abandoned and boarded up, so too was a nearby cottage. The houses in the little hamlet of Inverey – which had crofters living in them 40 years ago – are now largely owned by incomers, regularly visited by deer.

What is the greater challenge for a new owner of Mar Lodge? The great advantage of conservation ownership is that it can provide continuity and the organisation involved may feel better able than a sporting landowner to look outside the crude subsidy system in deciding how to develop the land. And, in an area like the Cairngorms, it is less easy to dismiss conservation ownership as no more than the bourgeois twentieth-century equivalent of nineteenth-century sporting ownership: there are now no significant communities on the land or areas which would be suitable for repopulation in any significant way. In this situation, ownership directed primarily at conservation – rather than social and economic – values is a good bet.

In an attempt to influence the NTS, Dr Watson, retired chief scientist from the Institute of Terrestrial Ecology in Banchory, and the land use consultant and agricultural adviser, Drennan Watson, wrote in 1994 to Mr Hamish Leslie Melville, the Trust chairman. Not only are their views unlikely to attract dissension among the wider conservation movement throughout Britain, they are equally unlikely to find criticism internationally. (With flawed logic, some people have tried to have the Cairngorms designated as a World Heritage site of conservation importance, an accolade which applies only to St Kilda in Scotland. It would make no sense to designate such a degraded, abused and misused environment —attractive, and fascinating, though it remains to many people. Not yet, anyway.)

The first question posed by Watson and Watson is, 'What is the land used for?' They suggest that the question is already answered by the designation in 1954 of the Cairngorms National Nature Reserve, which defines the national and international interest.

Although the area of the reserve is limited to 17,000 acres of the estate, it would make sense to apply the same protection to the outer zone, as these areas ultimately decide the fate of the core area. Islands of biodiversity in a sea of degradation – the Site of Special Scientific Interest approach – are no longer seen as a sound strategy.

By the end of 1999, the Trust was already deeply engaged with its vision of an estate managed on conservation principles, but retaining its traditional sporting interests. So, while the same visiting shooters continued to enjoy stag or hind stalking, they had begun to see significant changes on the ground. Non-native tree species are being felled to prevent their regeneration, and deer fences have been taken down around the piecemeal plantations seemingly dropped on the landscape over the years. In the past, the fences kept the deer out of the trees and forced them to survive on the bare hill. Now they can use the plantations as a source of food and shelter. Where Scots pine has been planted, more fences are coming down and the edges of the new woods are being selectively felled, or 'feathered', to make them look more natural. And, importantly, the stalkers who were suspicious of Trust ownership have been won round, in the space of just a few years. They have seen the heather grow higher in the most heavily grazed parts of the estate, and detected signs of improving health in the deer herd. If these early positive indications are maintained and built upon, Mar Lodge could well become a model for other owners to adopt, and may help quell some of the fears of those lairds who believe conservation and deer management are separate issues.

Neighbouring estates feared that the heavy deer culls would create a vacuum and attract their herds on to Mar Lodge. But this has not happened. If anything, the intense culls have tended to push deer out of the estate.

Then there is the great lodge itself. When conservation groups take over estates, the Victorian mansion that comes with them invariably leads to much wringing of hands. The Trust's solution is commendable. It has turned the lodge into attractive self-catering apartments, with visitors enjoying communal access to the grand public rooms.

But there has been no national publicity drive and no attempt to attracts hordes of visitors to Mar Lodge. It has become the biggest single area in Britain managed for conservation, but it will not be turned into a commercially driven national park.

In fact, the Trust is making the land less accessible to some members of the public. It has discouraged the use of mountain bikes, for example, and keeps road gates padlocked to prevent people driving into the mountains.

In 1976, the key objective for the Cairngorms nature reserve was defined as 'the maintenance of near-natural evolutionary processes in the Cairngorms'. This would necessitate a pan-Cairngorms strategy for the land, involving the neighbouring estates. We are not yet at that stage of enlightenment, but we are, at last, getting closer to goals that were set more than 20 years ago, and then ignored.

Restoration of the land without the use of deer-fencing can be done. On Abernethy estate (the 42,000 acres owned by the RSPB on the other side of the Cairngorms), a heavy deer cull over successive years allowed the old pine woods to regenerate naturally, and the effects are dramatic and compelling. My first sight of a group of 30 stags in a vibrant pine forest, of mature heather, juniper, young birch, and healthy young pines beneath the old granny trees, was both stirring and striking. Striking because I had been used – from my boyhood in Glennachulish – to seeing large numbers of deer on the open moors of Glencoe and the Black Mount. Seeing them in the middle of a growing forest was instantly sensible, natural. They looked good. The environment looked good. And they used the cover of the trees to run away from us.

Inevitably, of course, restoring a troubled environment is never simple. On Mar Lodge there are mature larch and spruce populations, and if the pines flourish again, so will the non-native species. Then there is the prospect of the arrival of sika deer, the Oriental import which is hybridising with red deer in many areas, and the threat of the grey squirrel, which is already in lower Deeside.

The overall goal of 'near-natural evolution' will be no easy management task for the NTS, and one that it has not tried on any other property. As a result, Mar Lodge represents an unprecedented opportunity to enhance the reputation of the Trust, and to put fire in the cool heart of Scottish conservation.

We must hope the new owner is up to the task.

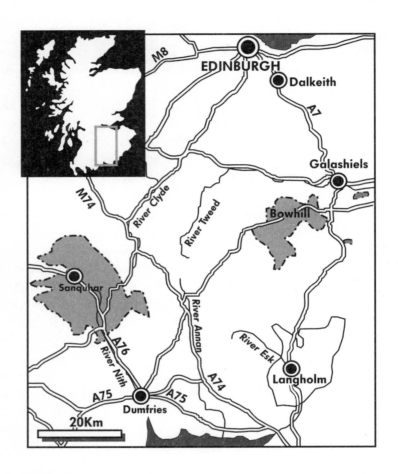

ACREAGE – 280,000 (INCLUDING 11,000 IN NORTHAMPTONSHIRE)
OWNERS – DUKE OF BUCCLEUCH, EARL OF DALKEITH
MANAGED FOR – FORESTRY, FARMING, SPORT
POINTS OF INTEREST – BIGGEST PRIVATE ESTATE IN BRITAIN:
DRUMLANRIG, ONE OF FIVE ESTATES, IS THE BIGGEST SINGLE
BLOCK OF ESTATE LAND OWNED IN UK

CHAPTER FOUR

Buccleuch Estate

T he rusting, tangled range of cars is visible over the wall. There is a digger working at one end of the pile and a narrow column of black smoke, the emblem of every scrapyard, rising at the other. A few plants on top of the stone wall appear to be grey in colour, caught between traffic and the metal graveyard.

At the roundabout there is a small shack called Jaws Takeaway and a rundown church hall with a sign above the door declaring, Beds Direct. Then there are two red-brick houses, incongruous in the commercial jungle. In one of them lives the widow of the harbourmaster. Thanks to the finger of the paternal landowner – akin to the hand of fate used to advertise the lottery – she pays no rent.

These, and many other unlikely properties in scruffy Granton, on the edge of Edinburgh and the River Forth, belong to Buccleuch estates. It is the smoking scrapyard, the Christian Salvesen cold store, the shortbread-making unit and the double-glazing business which help sustain the rural grandeur of Scotland's greatest surviving land-owning family. The multiplicity of small industrial units here, and in one or two other sites in the city, help pay for the grouse-stalking and the salmon-fishing, and made a significant contribution towards the £1 million restoration of the roof of Drumlanrig Castle – the stolid, luxurious mansion which is one of four properties regularly inhabited by the Duke and Duchess of Buccleuch.

Just 50 acres of down-at-heel Granton act as a vital cash cow for 280,000 country acres in the Scottish Borders and Northamptonshire. Without the corner shops, the terraced houses and the city entrepreneurs anxious to start out in business, Buccleuch would not be such a profitable enterprise.

As it is, with a policy of increasing its business interests in Edinburgh – selling in scruffy areas and buying into better industrial properties – it is a remarkable oddity in the world of land-owning today. It is already more than twice the size or the next biggest estate, and it is growing. And it makes money.

On a quick Range Rover tour of the site, Buccleuch estate's chief executive Michael Clarke, formerly chief land agent to the Ministry of Defence, explains the attractions and the problems. 'This is high-risk stuff. You get people who don't pay their rents, or go bust. They may not always be the type of people you would want as neighbours, but it is a cash cow which doesn't stand us in very much. It is yielding into double figures.' Double figures feature prominently in the discussion as we visit the urban estate and its multifarious commercial units.

'We don't like it particularly, it doesn't give the same pleasure as buying a forest or buying a farm, there isn't the same convergence of interest between the occupier and the owner. We do it because we think it is important for survival. Properly managed, it can be something in which there is the pleasure of ownership.'

The Granton property has what Clarke calls 'a real miscellany of uses', and is, funnily enough, close to the duke's heart. Much of the Buccleuch property in Granton was compulsorily purchased after the last war, and His Grace remains aggrieved to this day, resentful that it has never been returned. Granton Harbour was built by the duke's great-great-grandfather in 1837, at his own expense and 'for the benefit of Edinburgh', according to the chief executive.

The industrial units are home to petfood and plumbing suppliers, a vehicle-repair centre and a taxi operator. Broompark Business Park, a small self-contained estate, includes a shortbread-maker to British Airways and a cable-television dealer. 'We borrowed money to buy this,' says Clarke, 'and we are paying it off over five years. There isn't much of a margin, but there is a margin, three or four per cent, and when we have cleared it, we will be getting double figures.'

The double-figure mantra does not apply when we pass a distinctive terrace on the shore, reminiscent of Wallsend and the north-east of England. Buccleuch used to own the lot, but today retains one or two of the houses, and expects little from them. 'The people are generally unemployed, drinking themselves silly, have built up huge arrears and know that the Duke of Buccleuch isn't going to take them to court.' The Range Rover passes without slowing.

He cites several examples of the risks associated with venturing out of the rural hinterland to manage the urban scene. 'A man has just gone back to Pakistan owing us a lot of money. He told us he was going to escape payment but we didn't believe him. However, we are left with rather a good shop, we might even get Kentucky Fried Chicken into it, which would be rather good.'

Imagine the envy with which the estate looks on Cameron Toll, where the shopping centre was sold at a profit of around £25 million within a few years of its opening. 'That would have made Buccleuch estate, but it would have been too risky. It is not something we would do.' It remains, however, constantly on the look-out. An application with Sainsbury's for a supermarket at Sheriffhall roundabout on the by-pass has been turned down. But Clarke believes more opportunities will come in the narrowing green gap between Edinburgh and Dalkeith. 'The green belt,' he remarks, 'is a dynamic thing.'

Much like the estate itself.

When you come over the rise on the A7009, on the southern shoulder of the woollen town of Selkirk, you see, for the first time since leaving Edinburgh, a softer Borders. Stretching away down the Ettrick valley to your right is a rolling landscape of wood and farmland, a place which looks more natural than most of the landscape passed so far, and yet one which is almost entirely manufactured by generations of Buccleuch dukes and duchesses.

This place, one way or another, has borne since the twelfth century the stamp of the families which the Duke of Buccleuch, 77, represents today. During that reign, and over a period of 400 years beginning in the middles ages, the land was denuded of its natural forests, partly by the abbeys which held sway and cleared the trees for sheep pastures, and partly by the warring English and Scots, who between them burned the woodland to expose their enemies. But the days when Scotland's kings hunted stag and wild boar in the ancient Ettrick Forest have left no echoes in the valley. The original native forest now survives mainly as fragments of birch woodland. Here and there, in the odd cleft or gully on the hillside, in places out of reach of grazing animals, a lone tree survives, perhaps a clump of juniper or a single rowan.

The landscape has changed out of all recognition in four millennia. Four thousand years ago the hilltops above the Ettrick would have been covered in birch and willow, with dwarf shrubs and heather. The zone below that was characterised by birch, willow, rowan and some Scots pine and juniper. On the lower slopes, and on the better soils, was a thick, mixed woodland of oak, ash, elm, gean, hawthorn, hazel, bird cherry and alder. A place of enchantment, rich in wildlife. Home to wild animals long since extinct.

Today, the landscape has a youngish look to it. The hills which have fed millions of sheep since the sixteenth century have a washed-out-green aspect, and the woods – begun by Duchess Anne in the early eighteenth century – look good, yet unnatural.

I am visiting on a cold day in early March, with the blue skies and snow lingering on the hilltops and in the north-facing fields. The larch are clad in their attractive bracken colours, and the sitka spruce in the distance are dark green, with that characteristic blue caste, like a fine dust settled on hard needles. There are Norway spruce among them, and there are birch and even some grand Douglas fir.

This is a landscape of the past two centuries, thanks to the gambling ways of the fourth Duke of Queensberry, who lived his life and squandered his inheritance in London gambling dens in the late eighteenth century. He cut down the tress on the estate – planted by his predecessors – to pay his losses. The Buccleuch dukes have been made of stouter stuff since. The woods were replaced by the fifth duke, the great-great-grandfather of the present incumbent, who laid out the plantations to resemble the shadow of cumulus clouds on a sunny hillside.

Before reaching the Bowhill estate office, I stop to look across to the great house. From my vantage point on the gravelly floor of the valley I catch a glimpse of the sloping lawn in front of Bowhill. The treescape in the immediate vicinity is more attractive than the commercial plantations on the hill behind. The policy woodlands here – as on many other estates – form some of the most attractive woods in Scotland, an undoubted positive aspect of land-ownership – although some might resent the very deliberate beautification of their own surroundings by countless lords. Bowhill was built in 1812.

The Duke of Buccleuch is in residence at Bowhill in early March, where he signs himself, simply, Buccleuch. When he is staying at the great lump of Drumlanrig Castle in Dumfriess-shire he signs himself Buccleuch and Queensberry. He and the duchess flit around the estate homes, from art-stuffed mansion-house to mansion-house. The other homes are Boughton House in Northamptonshire, sometimes called the Versailles of England, Drumlanrig and his London residence. Dalkeith Palace, a popular family haunt 80 years ago, is today rented to the University of Wisconsin, which brings students to Scotland for a year at a time.

It is fair to say there is an awful lot of history in the name of John Montagu Douglas Scott, ninth Duke of Buccleuch and eleventh of Queensberry. His three surnames are those of the three land-owning families – Scott of Bowhill, Douglas of Drumlanrig, and Montagu of Boughton – united through marriage over the past 900 years. Remarkably, for the past 30 generations, the Scots succession has passed from father to son, with the single exception of the one daughter to inherit, Anne, Duchess of Buccleuch and Monmouth, who married the son of King Charles II in the middle years of the seventeenth century. This century, the present duke's father married Mary Lascelles, granddaughter of the tenth Duke of St Albans, and therefore – like her husband – a direct descendant of Charles II, but through Nell Gwynne.

Down through the years, plum lands have been acquired by marriage and inheritance, to complete the shape of Buccleuch estates at the turn of the millennium. The sheer scale of the enterprise is emphasised by the fact that one of the five estates, Queensberry, centred on Drumlanrig Castle, is 110,000 acres in size, and the biggest single block of privately owned land in Britain today. At 280,000 acres, Buccleuch estates are twice the size of the next biggest landholding in Britain, and half the size they were just 70 years ago.

The duke, who has been confined to a wheelchair since breaking his back in a riding accident in 1971, is an unashamed self-publicist and a great defender of the merits of good commercial forestry, and of the virtues of the landowner. He takes the defence of private estates to the extreme.

Shortly after our brief meeting at Bowhill, he wrote to me in order to venture 'one or two thoughts which may not have been covered'. Firstly, he let me know that nearly all the landowners used as bad examples of the breed had come from abroad, 'to fill the vacuum formed by traditional estate owners who had been driven out of business by excessive taxation which has crippled and fragmented large numbers of estates throughout most of this century'.

This attack on the landed was the fault of what the former Tory MP calls 'pink politicians' who thought landowners were an obstacle to progress. 'Perhaps they were at that time, but the barons of industry took over at least 60 to 70 years ago. This fact has escaped the notice of politicians of all parties, since they are almost all townsmen ignorant of country affairs, right up to today.

'Although the Great British public bemoan the decline of the countryside in terms of beauty and environmental protection, people are simply unaware of the cause and effect – the reduction, in one lifetime, of the proportion of land managed by traditional estates from over 90 per cent to under 30 per cent.'

This last statement jars, somewhat, with the reputation of Buccleuch estates as a place where birds of prey were routinely, and illegally, killed to protect grouse-shooting. However, the estate has since banned persecution of birds of prey on its land and has taken part in a joint project with conservationists to study the effect on commercial grouse moors of undisturbed birds of prey. The project proved that hen harriers can devastate grouse populations on grassy moors, but a follow-up project showed that artificial feeding could stop raptors eating the game birds.

His letter continues with the sweeping statement that without the demise of the traditional landowner, estates like Mar Lodge would not be the subject of soul-searching today. And he takes a swipe at the National Trust for Scotland. 'If the previous owners had not been crippled by tax burdens, there would have been no need for rescue and management by the National Trust, which costs the taxpayer far more and reduces historic house atmosphere to that of Waverley Station.

'In summary, traditional rural estates, far from being a feudal anachronism, are being shown daily to be the best way of harmonising the often conflicting interests of the countryside to the advantage of farming, forestry, wildlife, recreation and, above all, to the rural communities who live there.'

So there.

This estate is different. The Bowhill estate office is noticeably warm. At the weekend the office is heated by oil, during the week – like Blair Castle – its piped water is warmed by wood from the estate forests. Several months into my research for this book, I have at last escaped from the swirling draughts of the big empty mansions and the poorly insulated estate buildings. I have also escaped from the penniless lairds.

It is different in many ways. Although the duke was an active Conservative MP for Edinburgh North from 1960–73, and has been a tireless campaigner on forestry standards and environmental education, there is something that sets him, and his son, Richard, Earl of Dalkeith, apart from many Highland landowners: their estates make money.

The duke and the earl have enjoyed highly successful careers but they were not forced to make a crust in London, and they have tended to be less absent than most Scottish landowners. Although they both have London homes, they spend as much time as possible at their respective Scottish houses – the duke and the duchess (daughter of John McNeill of Colonsay, one of the oldest Scottish families) vacillating between the mansions, and the earl at his home of Dabton, by Drumlanrig. 'It is the antithesis of absenteeism,' says chief executive Michael Clarke.

It is difficult to grasp the scale of the estate enterprises. Richard Dalkeith remarks that I am not covering much of the Borders country in this book, but Buccleuch, in its separate holdings, stretches from city centre Edinburgh to the fringes of Dalkeith, to Selkirk, to Dumfriess-shire and, at Langholm, to the English border. It adds up to an area equivalent to three of the biggest Highland estates, and enjoys better land – even though Lord Dalkeith points out that 95 per cent of the land is designated as disadvantaged.

Bowhill, at 46,000 acres, employs 64 people full time, eight part time, and together the estates employ at least 250 individuals, or as many as 1,000 if contractors and other related jobs are considered. The whole area (home farms and 200 let farms) sends 130,000 lambs and 14,000 cattle to market or abattoir each year, and produces 20,000 tonnes of cereals and potatoes and 20 million litres of milk. There are 1,200 houses on the land – a quarter of them are listed buildings, and a quarter are lived in rent free by employees or retired employees. The forests produce 50,000 tonnes of timber and there are more than 5,000 miles of stone walls, hedges and fences. This is just a part of the story.

Excluding Granton, the estates are:

BOWHILL

The house is a mile above the confluence of the Ettrick and Yarrow rivers, two of the main tributaries of the Tweed. It includes the ruins of Newark Castle, once used as a hunting lodge by the kings of Scotland. The house dates from 1812, with no visible trace of the original building which was erected in 1780. During the nineteenth century the grounds were landscaped and two lochs were excavated. It is open to the public from May to August.

DRUMLANRIG

Also known as the Queensberry estate, is situated in the valley of the River Nith. Part of the estate was derived from King Robert Bruce, whose right-hand man was Sir James Douglas of Drumlanrig. The castle was built of local sandstone during 1679–91 on the site of an old Douglas stronghold and is regarded as an important renaissance building. Approximately 88 per cent of the surrounding 110,000-acre Nithsdale estate is tenanted farms, with just 3,000 acres of in-hand farm concentrating on dairy farming. The dairy farm provides 50 per cent of the income. The 10,000 acres of forestry are a great love of the duke and the castle policies have a number of specimen trees, including the biggest sycamore in Britain. The castle and grounds are open from May to August for an average of 35,000 visitors.

LANGHOLM

Also known as Eskdale and Liddesdale estate, it covers 94,000 acres from the English border to Hawick. Once Douglas territory, the lands were confiscated when the Douglases quarrelled with King James II and were defeated at the Battle of Arkinholm (now Langholm) in 1455. Much of the land was then acquired by the Scotts. The mansion for the estate was Branxholm Castle, which is now tenanted.

There are over 10,000 acres of forestry, 90 tenanted farms and 200 tenanted houses. It was the site of a pioneering study into the effects of birds of prey on grouse.

DALKEITH

Covering 2,500 acres on the outskirts of Edinburgh, Dalkeith has been in the Buccleuch family for almost 600 years. There was an interlude in the family's ownership when the estate was sold to Charles I, who in 1637 enclosed the parklands which can be seen today as a hunting ground. However, the property was bought back in 1642 by Francis Scott, second Earl of Buccleuch, whose younger daughter, Anne, married the Duke of Monmouth, natural son of Charles II – they were created the Duke and Duchess of Buccleuch. In the early eighteenth century, Dalkeith Palace was described as the 'grandest of all early classical houses in Scotland'. The laundry has recently been converted and is occupied by Scottish Natural Heritage.

BOUGHTON
The Northamptonshire property came to the Buccleuchs through the marriage of Elizabeth Montagu to Henry, third duke of Buccleuch, fifth Duke of Queensberry, in the late eighteenth century. The house is the result of a 250-year transformation of a fifteenth-century monastic building. It is little changed since 1700 when it was given its château appearance by a devotee of French architecture. It covers 11,000 acres, most of it in a protected landscape area. A total of 3,700 acres is farmed in hand, with 13 let farms and 2,200 acres of woodland. It is open to the public in August, and during the year for special educational visits.

The houses themselves are treasure troves of art collected over the centuries. Paintings include the celebrated *Madonna with the Yarnwinder* by Leonardo da Vinci, and works by Rembrandt, Canaletto, Raeburn, Gainsborough and Ruysdael.

To keep things simple, I am concentrating on Bowhill, of which Sir Walter Scott wrote:

> When summer smiled on sweet Bowhill,
> And July's eve, with balmy breath,
> Waved the bluebells on Newark-heath;
> When throstles sung in Harehead shaw,
> And corn was green on Carterhaugh,
> And flourished, broad, Blackandro's oak,
> The aged Harper's soul awoke!

Buccleuch estates have an open-house policy for the press, and plenty of staff to interview. Waiting in the estate office are Lord Dalkeith, Michael Clarke, and the Bowhill factor (each estate has its own) Niall Campbell.

Buccleuch Estates Ltd was formed in 1923, the year the present duke was born. He enjoys telling people that he does not own a single acre in Scotland, although he is chairman of the company. Technically he is correct, but then again, very few landowners in Scotland own their land as one might own a house. Most properties are in trusts in order to avoid punitive death duties. Of course, if the land is sold, the money goes to the main beneficiaries.

The mission statement is laudable: to care for the countryside, to sustain the estates, and to improve public understanding of, and access to, the countryside.

Richard Dalkeith – its shorter than Richard Walter John Montagu Douglas Scott – former chairman of the south-west regional board of the Scottish Natural Heritage and a member of the Millennium Commission – is a youthful 44, although the reddish hair is receding. He speaks with just a hint of a lisp and a mansion-house accent via Eton and Christ Church, Oxford.

Clarke, a tall, bespectacled man of ruddy complexion – redolent of a regiment – tells me the policy on Buccleuch land is based on the initials VSE. They stand for value, stewardship and education.

Value means a sound commercial base, without which it is not possible to practise the second goal of good stewardship. (Although those present would not like to put it this way, this statement from a successful lowland estate is an admission of the fact that Highland estates do not work terribly well because they have no sound commercial base.)

Education is about helping people to understand the estate and the way it works, whether schoolchildren, students, tenant farmers, or visiting journalists. We are all welcome (another lesson for the Highlands).

'You won't hear people talking about biodiversity or the Earth Summit here, but that is what we have been doing,' says Clarke. 'The two principal reasons we manage to do it are the family's commitment to this as a business and their willingness to see the money ploughed back and reinvested, year after year. There is a commitment to the inheritance, a common inheritance of all those involved on the estate.

'If this estate was broken up, it would be the end of life as we know it. This is an engine of labour creation, a large number of jobs would not exist without it. The returns are no more than one or two per cent, which makes it one of the most selfless forms of asset ownership you can get. If it was a monolith, if it was selfish, I could understand criticism. But it is a way of keeping families, and people and communities going. The estate is not run at their expense.' The estate is well enough aware of criticisms levelled at the landed gentry. Criticisms which are enjoying something of a revival.

Lord Dalkeith, like many lords and dukes of modern Scotland, is deeply proud of his family history.

'We could all be living the life of Reilly in the south of France, but we have been around for rather a long time and we want to be around a bit longer. I feel a very powerful sense of inheritance, of ten or 12 generations who go back on this land and who have done their best. That is a pretty strong motivating factor. I feel very emotionally attached to the land, I mind very much about that.

'It is not unreasonable for people to express their views on the way land is managed. It is reasonable for people to question, particularly given all the public subsidies, the quality of the management and its priorities. I am not afraid of it, because I think we do it okay.'

Dalkeith's father has recognised the vital role of education in attempting to win support. Those estates which hide from the limelight, which attempt to ignore developments in the outside world, whether at Rio or at Selkirk, are the ones which are most immediately threatened.

'No one is going to get back to the time 200 or 300 years ago when everything revolved around a large house. But a lot of history and a place of some importance like Buccleuch estates should be part of the community. We have to look outwards. We have to think about what people outside think about what we are doing. We really have to relate to the local community interests.'

It is easy to view the Buccleuch estates as the best sort of paternalism on the land. Some of the estate families can be traced back as long as the owners, and many workers today will spend their entire working lives toiling for His Grace.

In an effort to prove just how popular his regime is, the duke conducted an anonymous poll of 125 farm tenants in 1993. When asked whether they considered the present system to be fair, quite fair or unfair, only eight per cent opted for the last option. And when asked what sort of landlord they would prefer, 96 per cent said a private family company, or a family.

Was this a fair test of the value of the landowner today? Hardly. Of the 125 tenants, 44 per cent had inherited their leases – and a way of life – and 56 per cent had become tenants by application. They were, as it were, bound to say that. When asked how they would advise a young man with £100,000 to enter farming, an overwhelming 89 per cent said 'rent a farm'. It is highly likely, however, that the duke and the sprawling estate machine are, at least, generally popular.

The estate is to be commended for the fact that, in some areas, it is not simply dedicated to profit. It is planting hedgerows, using the appropriate facing brick in renovations, putting in fencing which follows contours. It would be easier simply to make money. Clarke insists the policy is to take a long view of things, which means the prospective estate farmer with good intentions will be preferred to the less reliable applicant offering more money.

The houses are free to the staff for the duration of their lives and most of them are centrally heated – a rare thing on a big estate. 'I don't know any other estate that does that sort of thing to the same extent,' remarks Clarke.

So Buccleuch is a great, sprawling, all-enveloping benevolent dictatorship (the estate would rather describe it as a co-operative). It provides sumptuous accommodation for the duke, a privileged lifestyle for the earl, and jobs and produce for countless others. It is trying to bridge the gap in understanding between the town and the country. It wants to have Buccleuch become part of the curriculum at the local schools; it is progressive, it is dedicated to diversification, and it carries out improvements with its tenants on a 50-50 basis.

And so the list goes on. Buccleuch estates are run in a businesslike fashion, with two highly political men in charge. The duke was for many years an MP, and Lord Dalkeith stood as a prospective parliamentary candidate for the Tories, and as a councillor. It seems his political ambitions, unlike those of his father, are limited by a modern climate in which the laird is no longer seen as a representative of the people, not even by the Tory party.

If the duke has a passion in countryside matters then it is forestry. He is also adept at publicity. In *The Field* in January 1993, a generous headline writer dubbed him 'The One-Man National Trust'; in *Country Life* in January 1995, he was 'The Duke of Buccleuch, Forestry Expert'.

He is a great promoter of the value of commercial forestry, bemoaning the fact that nine out of ten trees used in the timber industry in Britain are imported, and has little time for native woodland regeneration if it is to be promoted at the expense of a good, mixed forestry plantation with a commercial crop. Forestry management on the estate today includes management for game, nature conservation, recreation and access, although the current motivation is highly commercial. Much more so than it was in the post-war years.

The duke will reel off the positive virtues of sitka spruce and larch, which will produce a return in 40 to 50 years, and has made videos to expound his own views on the failure of government subsidies, and of the urgent need for a much higher level of planting in Scotland. The national balance of payments, he says in a video with David Bellamy, suffers from the fact that timber is one of Britain's biggest imports, costing £1 million every 75 minutes. He values native species in their place, he remains more interested in sound commercial business.

This view appears to exclude the possibility that, in the long term, a processing industry could evolve to use native broad-leaved trees and Scots pine. At present the industry is stuck on sitka because it matures in 40 instead of 80 years.

Over a whisky in the library, a room of generous proportions made habitable by the clutter and the magazines and drink bottles – the bookshelves do not quite reach the ceiling, leaving a strip for family portraits around the room – the duke expresses doubt that the native pinewoods being encouraged by Forestry Commission grants will ever produce commercially useful timber.

'You must be able to produce consistent crops of timber and this must be done in a way that is environmentally sensitive, with sufficient open spaces, sufficient mixture of age groups and different species. It is best for wildlife, best for scenery.' And, he adds with feeling, 'You have to make sure you are not going to invade your neighbours with all kinds of raptors and vermin.'

Earlier, on a tour of Bowhill with Lord Dalkeith and the chief executive, we stopped at about the 1,000ft contour, between the Ettrick and Yarrow valleys, for a meeting with head keeper Brian Johnson. There was a dusting of snow on the short-cropped heather, and a cold wind which invited Johnson into the back of the Range Rover. On the south side of the hill we were looking at an area managed by a tenant and damaged by the heavy grazing of cattle and sheep. Several years ago, the estate gave the farmer £8,000 as an inducement to take stock off the hill in an effort to retrieve the heather. As a result of this conservation-minded action, the farmer's rent had to be reduced by £5,000 a year.

'I find it incredibly difficult to get it across to people how scarce and valuable our heather resource is,' says Lord Dalkeith from the driving seat. 'Heather is an island in the part of Scotland we are talking about.' His real concern is the dwindling stock of grouse, the shooting of which should be a useful income for the estate. He blames the Forestry Commission for failing to control predators in neighbouring forestry blocks, and adds that raptors 'have been given the run of the place'.

Johnson clearly disagrees with the protection of all birds of prey on a grouse moor. He expects the winter kill by peregrine falcons to be 'enormous', but adds, in reference to the estate's pro-raptor policy (which has won a lot of positive publicity): 'We know where we stand. At the kennels the other day there were ten buzzards circling around. They are said to mainly take carrion and rabbits, but I have seen them take grouse and full-grown pheasants.'

Although the RSPB regularly quotes Buccleuch as a great supporter of its campaign against illegal persecution, particularly of the main grouse predators, the hen harrier and the peregrine falcon, there seems to be pretty unanimous agreement on the scale of the problem.

Clarke says: 'We know jolly well there is a strong case for culling and having control of the population of some of these raptors. They breed in other countries, while the poor grouse is unique to this country. But because it is thought to be a rich man's sport, those who subsidise the RSPB and others are simply not interested in defending it.'

Other birdlife is positively encouraged, with owl perches erected in woodland plantations, and the resident forester on Bowhill went so far as to suggest that every wood should have its goshawk. A comment, I'd wager, which caused the duke to raise his eyebrows.

What conclusion can be reached about such a vast empire? For all its enormity, the Buccleuch system illustrates a lot of the positive arguments for estate ownership. Commercial forestry has been more sensitively executed here than on many other estates, or by many private woodland companies. The intensification of agriculture which removed wetland and took fields to the boundary fence at the expense of biodiversity, has not been allowed on every corner of Buccleuch estates. The property does look at design issues and landscaping in its decisions, and the landowners are active in public life and committed to explaining why they are the best guardians of the countryside. There has been continuity in the management of the land.

In June 1994, the duke wrote an article in *Country Living* to debunk the notion that landowners were, in his words, 'feudal-minded, port-sodden old hermits potting pheasants and putting up keep-out signs'. He declared himself responsible for 430 square miles of beautiful landscaped countryside, and the people and wildlife it supports.

'Contrary to popular belief, landowners do not have limitless funds. The majority would only be immensely wealthy – that label so popular with the tabloid press – if they sold their land and stopped being landowners. Even the space taken by a wastepaper basket in a

London office is more valuable than a whole acre in the northern hillsides.'

He cites the provision of access opportunities, the work of educational trusts, nature conservation programmes and enlightened management techniques as proof of how necessary landowners are today. He and his son, he points out, have been through the hoops of calving, lambing, fence building and tree planting. But in these leftish times, he has found himself fighting a losing battle against land reform and, in the autumn of 1999, against the loss of voting rights for hereditary peers in the Lords. The duke was one of those who lost their place in the Upper House.

Nevertheless the duke remains a significant figure in Scotland, with a deal of influence in the worlds of art, forestry and politics. Buccleuch estates are all but a household name, and he has managed, at a difficult time for landowners, to maintain a positive image.

But in strict environmental terms, there are too many sheep on the hills, there is too little biodiversity in the commercial forests and native woodland is almost non-existent. The rivers are suffering from a lack of management. As elsewhere, there are rumours that raptors are still killed and there is no shortage of heather cropped to a stubble.

If the public is to find fault, then it is more likely to be founded on an individual distaste for omnipotent ownership itself. Are all those mansions, those endless hills and forests and farms best owned by one family?

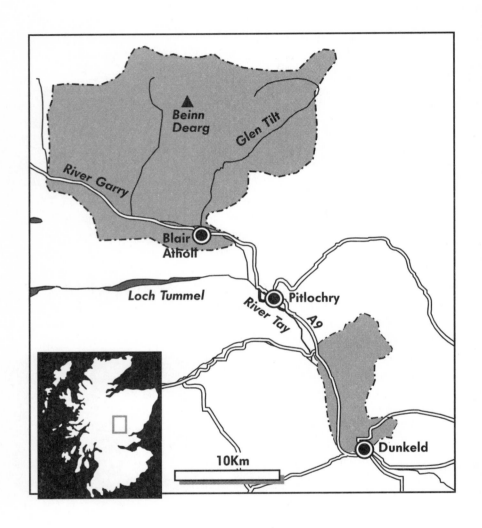

ACREAGE – 130,000
OWNER – SARAH TROUGHTON, BLAIR CHARITABLE TRUST
MANAGED FOR – TOURISM, FORESTRY, FARMING, SPORT
POINTS OF INTEREST – ON DUKE'S DEATH, TITLE AND LAND
WERE SEPARATED. TITLE PASSED TO SOUTH AFRICAN.

CHAPTER FIVE

Atholl Estate

There is a Disneyland feel to Blair Atholl, as if the clean, grey granite façades were not quite the real thing. For a start, it is unusual in a Highland village to see a main street lacking the garish signs and shouting advertisements which are taken to extremes in, for example, Tyndrum. Blair is oddly tasteful for a Highland village, if you like your villages homogeneous. It looks as if it is all part of one enterprise, and it is.

It was built by successive Dukes of Atholl, the two hotels are estate partnerships, and many of the houses are still rented from the estate. There is even a caravan and camping park, built on natural terraces, which manages not to offend the eye and from where it is possible to leave your tent and wander next door into the grounds of one of Scotland's most attractive historic houses.

Then there is the castle itself, a whitewashed, turreted affair which conforms to the American ideal; it is almost Hearst-esque in its grand setting when seen from the A9 on the other side of the River Garry. It nestles below dark green hills, its flag flying despite the fact that the last Scottish duke, George Iain Murray, who lived in converted servants' quarters, died in 1996. The eleventh duke, his distant cousin, is a land surveyor in South Africa.

Those travellers casting an envious glance towards the castle while heading south have been on estate land since four miles north of Calvine, and will remain inside the boundaries until Dunkeld, a distance of 20 miles. Once you know what to look for, the estate cottages and farms are not hard to recognise – a total of 280 rented properties and 20 tenanted farms. They mainly conform to the nineteenth-century Blair style.

And yet, despite the very public countenance of the estate, very little is known about it. Indeed, the estate has rarely bothered over the years to correct the same inaccuracies that have been repeated time and again in almost any article written about the place and its late duke.

He was described as the owner of Atholl's 130,000 acres. In fact, he had never, since inheriting at the age of 26, been the sole owner. The land had always been shared by 'Wee Iain' – as the press dubbed the 6ft 5in laird – and his mother's family.

The duke's half-sister, Sarah Troughton (née Campbell-Preston), wife of the London architect, Jamie, holds the 18,000-or-so acres known as the Dunkeld and Middle District stretching north from Dunkeld on the east side of the A9. Before his death, the duke owned no more than two or three thousand acres around the castle. The rest, more than 100,000 acres in one great square shape backing into the hills, was held in trust. The bachelor duke was a trustee, but not the main beneficiary. Most of the land was gifted by him to the Blair Charitable Trust which aims to generate enough money to sustain itself. Any profit that accrues is distributed to other charities.

On the duke's death, the title that had jumped from distant cousin to distant cousin because of a remarkably consistent failure by successive dukes to father an heir, passed to a South African cousin, John Murray. He did not get the castle or the land along with the title, but does have the use of a flat and can boast to his friends in South Africa that he has his own private army back home in Scotland, However, he rarely visits Scotland and the estate seems rather sad without an unmarried duke to arouse media curiosity, attract criticism and open fêtes.

As is to be expected, the newspapers that love to bash a laird have, since 1996, gone rather quiet on the subject of the Atholl estate. And the *Sunday Times* can no longer list the tenth duke as one of Britain's richest men while passing the wry but tired comment that he was also one of the country's most eligible bachelors. 'He was not one of Britain's richest men,' the factor Andrew Gordon told me with finality.

He was, however, in the words of one of his employees, 'a useful consolidator'.

He maintained the estate in very much the traditional style, with no great innovation in land management or operation. He remained, however, greatly interested in the detail. In many areas he continued the good work carried out by Angela Pearson, the mother he shared with Sarah Troughton, who effectively ran Atholl estate – with no public profile – until her death in 1981. It was only then that the duke, who had been pursuing a career in London with the *Westminster Press*, the family newspaper business from his mother's side, became more involved.

Sarah Troughton, more approachable than her late brother, visits the place regularly and has done since she was a girl. But she finds it hard to imagine living there full time. The last duke, who suffered ill health for several years before his stroke at Christmas in 1995, spent more and more time at Blair. I visited the estate the year before he died, and found him to be extremely shy. Yet friends told me he was very sharp, a stout defender of private ownership, and a good committee chairman. He was, for example, chairman of *Westminster Press*, and president of the Royal National Lifeboat Institute. But, in common with his predecessors, and despite the claims of the press, he was not fabulously wealthy. The ninth duke left £320,000. The wealth lies not in the individual's bank balance but in the land and property, which make very little profit. The same could be said for most estates owned by old families.

Living in Blair Castle might seem to be significant luxury. But the reality is that life in the large staterooms would not be particularly comfortable, unless the resources were available to install double glazing, a new heating system and insulation. The duke's relatively modest quarters made much more sense than the grand hall.

My abiding memory of researching this book is of cold feet, slowly chilled by the ever-present low-level swirl of an unseen icy grip which begins life as a merest wisp at one end of a great building and mutates into a good-going breeze by the time it finds human occupants at the other.

Atholl is no different to many of the big traditional estates in failing to cover its costs. And yet the owners hang on to the land with a stubborn regard for the place, for history and the privilege of ownership.

In the estate offices at Blair, and in the small room at the back of the castle occupied by archivist Jane Anderson, the same old story came through. There may be, in the public's mind, an imagined solidity about these great tracts of land but the truth is that their survival has rarely been a foregone conclusion.

That Atholl estate exists as it does today is due entirely to one individual – Angela Pearson's grandmother, the redoubtable Annie, Lady Cowdray, of Cowdray Park in England and Dunecht Estate in Aberdeenshire. The crucial date in the modern history of Atholl was 31 July 1931.

The shortened version of a rather romantic tale goes like this. In the 1930s, Atholl, in common with other estates, was feeling the pinch of depression. Debts were mounting and the Union Bank of Scotland in Glasgow was growing increasingly impatient with the eighth duke's indebtedness. The duke, conscious of the weight of history and the Murray family inheritance, had no intention of selling the whole estate.

Instead, he embarked on a succession of strange enterprises, each one characterised by outrageous optimism and hubris. He decided, for example, on a singular use for the large amounts of surplus steel which had become available on struggling Clydeside. He would build steel houses.

He bought a large quantity of metal and did indeed build steel houses, some of which are still standing today. He expanded the enterprise to France, and then moved on to Rumania where he was given a contract for 80,000 metal homes. The first expansion fell around his ears largely because of lack of orders, the second because the Rumanians could not afford to pay.

Then there was an ill-fated involvement in the Anglo-Argentine Tramways company. The duke became a director and hoped to make his fortune from the expansion of the rail network – until political upheaval changed the rules and took a dim view of foreigners making money in Argentina.

All was not lost: he was also involved in the Jamaica Sugar Estates. That venture failed with the falling price of sugar.

This Atholl laird had a wonderful knack, proven time and again, of getting into a venture at just the wrong time. In 1929, he went to Egypt to meet the royal family and the prime minister, on behalf of the Docker Heinemann Company, to persuade them to raise the Aswan dam in order to electrify Egypt. He returned well satisfied with his meetings, confident that his monetary problems would soon be over. The Egyptian Government collapsed.

Along the way, through the late 1920s, he sold off bits of the estate here, bits there. He ate into chunks of a once much larger empire – Dalnacardoch went, Glenshee went, Riechip and others went over the years.

His nadir was the month of July 1931, when the Union Bank was pressing for repayment of his overdraft and for a bond of security over the estate itself. It was at this point that Annie Lady Cowdray came to the rescue.

The Atholls and the Cowdrays had met socially during the 1920s and the relationship was sealed with the marriage in 1930 of Lady Cowdray's granddaughter, Angela (the mother of the present duke), to the dashing Tony Murray.

It seemed likely to Lady Cowdray that Lt. Col. George Anthony Murray, although a third cousin twice removed, would ultimately fall heir to the Atholl estate and take his place as the tenth duke. The eighth duke, after all, was in his fifties and had produced no children, and his heir, Lord James Murray, was of a similar age and unmarried. Tony was second in line.

Atholl's debts in 1930 ran to nearly £150,000. Significantly, he thought a proposal from Lady Cowdray to overhaul the management of Atholl 'much too businesslike', and so his doubts and prevarications delayed agreement until March 1932, when the bankers returned.

At that point there was no option and an agreement was signed to create Atholl Estates Limited, with Annie Cowdray investing £150,000, holding all the preference shares and having full control of the company. The duke had signed away his land.

The document was witnessed by Lady Cowdray on 10 March, and ten days later, after a minor operation, she left for Paris. On the night of 14 April she died unexpectedly, leaving the arrangements for the company incomplete, and leaving a large surprise for her son, Lord Cowdray. He knew nothing about her agreement, or the fact that she had spent £150,000 of the family's money as a long-term investment for her granddaughter, Lord Cowdray's daughter.

The story should be a film script. Tony Murray and Angela Pearson were never able to enjoy the estate together. He was killed in action in Italy in April 1945, shortly before the end of the war. By that time, the ninth duke was in position, having inherited in 1942, and he lasted until 1957, when Angela and Tony might have enjoyed the fruits of grandma's work. Instead, the title went to their only son, George Iain Murray – the last Scottish duke. Sarah Campbell-Preston, the only child of Angela Pearson's second marriage, inherited in 1974.

When the duke died, the land went out of Murray ownership – 'I do not have an ounce of Murray blood in me,' remarks Mrs Troughton – for the first time in over 360 years, ending a remarkable era which began in the early seventeenth century when one Dorothea Stewart (Atholl was originally Stewart land) married into the Murrays of Tullibardine.

Sarah Troughton, a boyish 40-something, attractive, with bobbed brown hair, in brown cord trousers, a bottle green polo-neck and a grey waistcoat, showed me to a foot-numbing room in the estate office. In a brief interview, she was straightforward, credible, uncomplicated.

We met during her Christmas break at Blair Atholl, a habit which she has transferred from her own childhood to her own children. Children, not surprisingly, love Blair Castle. She has a modern view of land-owning and its duties, and admits to a certain reticence over the role of the landowner. 'When I am in the middle of London, as I am most of the time, I don't go around shouting about how many acres I own, or the fact that I like shooting deer. Both are considered highly suspect. But when you ask am I uncomfortable with it, I am not. I think there is a shyness about it because I was taught, not that it is wrong to own a lot, but to be modest, for example, about what you own or earn. There is a debate about private land-ownership which goes on. There is bound to be a debate. People are always aware of who owns what, who earns what.'

I pointed out that in Scotland the exact opposite was part of the reason for the comdemnation of land ownership – people very definitely do not know who owns what.

Mrs Troughton finds her conscience 'feels better' because she believes that the more environmentally balanced parts of the countryside are those encompassed by big estates. But she illustrated the point in unusual fashion.

'If you have a very big estate you can take a more balanced view when you have pressure to house people. You have more to choose from, you can make a better choice. If you have a small estate and you are trying to keep it going, it can be tough, you can be under pressure to sell bits of land. If Britain was full of small-holdings it would be far more developed, in a more scattered and random way.

'I do get put under a lot of pressure to sell a little bit of land here, a little bit there. By and large I resist it. Although I have often sold sites on the edges of villages where the area plan has designated [development].'

Her point is unusual because she used as a defence of ownership the ability to resist housing development in the countryside. This reluctance to encourage scattered development – other than estate development – is highly unpopular with estate critics. There is, after all, a housing crisis in much of rural Scotland, due in part to local authority guidelines on development in the countryside, to incomers being able to pay higher prices than the indigenous populations, and due to the resistance of landowners.

Mrs Troughton is involved in two Scottish estates – Atholl, and her father's estate at Ardchattan Priory near Oban. She was, she said, 'as nervous of public ownership as of private', and quoted the example of her father selling land at a low price to the Forestry Commission in the 1950s, on the basis that it was the right thing to do. Now, the same Commission was trying to sell the land as part of its ongoing disposals programme and her family was worried about who was going to buy a chunk of forestry next door.

'I don't think myself that any solution is absolutely safe, really. Probably the answer is a balance of ownership. On Atholl estate the management will continue as much as it does now. The office maintains the whole estate, whether it belongs to me, or to a trust.

On a day-to-day basis, the estate is run by the factor, who has more immediate impact – and tends to be the butt of stronger criticism – than the landowners. It is the character of the factor which to a large extent determines the attitude of the community to the estate itself. It is up to the factor, for example, to review rents every three years.

Andrew Gordon, blunt but accessible, is not just the factor of Atholl estates. He is a landowner at neighbouring Lude estate, owns a deer forest at Glen Quoich on the west coast, and also factors Black Mount estate for another landowner.

He gives the impression he is sure of his ground and his opinions, willing to listen, but unlikely to change his mind. He makes no particular effort to soften his statements for public consumption, not out of any clumsiness or inability, but out of a belief in what he is saying. A fact is a fact, with this factor.

His office was a little warmer, but no more luxurious than the spartan room where I met Sarah Troughton. He told the predictable story of a large traditional estate relying on tourism, forestry, farming and sport. There are no grandiose plans today, no echo of the eighth duke in Andrew Gordon's conservative management style. Like most of the Scottish countryside, the place is governed to a large extent by the availability of farming grants decreed by Europe, by forestry incentives offered by the Forestry Commission and by the vagaries of the tourist market. A significant initiative since Angela Pearson's time was the creation in 1971 of the caravan park. It, along with the castle, forms the financial backbone of the enterprise today as the only reliable profit-making legs of the estate. Blair is Scotland's most-visited castle, attracting around 160,000 visitors a year.

By the end of 1996, that income was supplemented by visitors being asked for the first time to pay for car parking and for walking in the estate policies. 'Everybody else does it,' remarked Gordon, 'I don't see why we should be any different.'

The estate was criticised in the press in 1995 for instituting a £5 charge for drivers using the seven-mile road up Glen Tilt. The charge had been in place for several years, but the story was recycled, and the press loves to have a go at wealthy owners. How dare the lairds ask for taxpayers' money to plant trees or carry out repairs?

The answer is simple. Grants are made available to land managers of all sizes and descriptions because of a grand plan, say, to increase production, or improve the environment. It would be ludicrous to exclude large estates from the equation. If they were excluded, they would not carry out the work and the grand plan would fail. Environmental, and other, solutions in Scotland have to include landowners. If we all want environmental improvements, then the estate has either to be paid to make them happen or may have to sell the odd painting or three, perhaps a small chunk of land, perhaps a few houses, to make them happen. And most likely it won't.

Gordon is bullish about such things. He believes the estate has been too public spirited in allowing people to drive up Glen Tilt. And, although he knows it is not an option, he would like to have the hills free of walkers and all other visitors for a six-week period at the height of the stag-stalking season in August and September.

'I hope we can manage access. But I see it coming that people may have to keep on fixed routes. At certain times, some areas may have to be closed for deer management purposes. I don't hold with the freedom to roam about, I don't think many people do.' The estate was planning to ask people to stick to certain routes during the stag-stalking, with open access the rest of the year.

The stalkers on Atholl estates – particularly Charlie Price, who lives in Glen Tilt on the most popular walking and mountain-biking route – all have tales to tell about the problems of acting as first-aid experts for walkers with blisters, and worse.

Gordon is firmly opposed to wild camping and fails to understand why SNH described it as a permissible activity. 'There are three bothies on the estate and there is wild camping within the vicinity of them. But they really need some form of latrine facility. It gets pretty horrific by the end of the summer. When the keeper is out with the sheepdog the first thing it does is goes and lies in human shit and rolls in it. It is not very nice in the back of a Land Rover on the way home.'

He believes hillwalkers and climbers should be obliged to have insurance which would cover the cost of any rescues, and might return money to estates for the maintenance of access routes. And he would like to see favourable tax regimes for estates which would remove the dreaded inheritance tax. It is not hard to see why a landowner and factor would like to make money from access and estate paths, at a time when it is so difficult to make the traditional business work.

Forestry on Atholl, currently stretching to over 8,000 commercial acres, has been important for the last 250 years, with a number of dukes taking an interest in planting different parts of the estate. The fourth duke, the 'planting duke', planted huge areas of larch at the beginning of the last century. He was another laird with a grand idea of how to make the estate pay: he built larch fishing-boats and ferries to prove that the exotic conifer could be as good as the traditional oak, which was fast running out. And he estimated that the millions of larch planted would lead to an estate income of as much as £15 million by the advent of the twentieth century. Unfortunately for him, warships were being made out of steel by the time the crop was ready, and a large proportion of the forest was destroyed in a great gale in 1887.

In many ways he was ahead of his time. He was an avid recorder of his thoughts and achievements. He wrote one paper on the woods indigenous to the Grampians and remarked – 170 years ago – that if the higher ground on the estate was enclosed, there was an immediate rise of birch, ash and alder. A useful early admission of the state of grazing on hill land, circa 1820. There are still too many sheep and deer on exactly the same land, and they have been allowed for these past 17 decades to go on extracting the goodness from the ground and, in some areas, precipitating erosion.

In the same paper, the planting duke mourned the missing Caledonian Forest – 'now almost entirely exhausted'. He listed the last remaining sites as those at the head of the Dee, on neighbouring Invercauld, at Glenmore and on Loch Rannoch. The same key areas struggling on today. He adds that in bare Glen Lyon there were 100,000 pine trees.

The remains of the pine roots, he records, were split into shreds and used as candles by country people. He blames fire as the main agent of destruction, being used principally to destroy wolves and to root out enemies hiding in woods, and the fact that pine had a low export value. 'The remains of the forests, after the destruction of wolves, have been improvidently wasted.' What was left after the fires was coppiced to provide bark for tanning.

Larch, his main bequest to the estate – some of his trees can be seen in the castle policies – played a significant part in local building. It was used for the floor and roof joists at the shooting lodge in Glen tilt, and provided the centres for the Dunkeld bridge. The duke remarked at the time that the creation of the bridge – the crossing had been made by ferry, a precarious business in heavy floods – was 'to the great advantage of the public, and to my own convenience and comfort'.

Dunkeld is the southern outpost of the estate – the seventh duke built Dunkeld House, now the Dunkeld House Hotel, and bought numerous prominent buildings in the village. Marriages and deaths were marked at Dunkeld Cathedral.

Gordon commented that while the modern forestry effort included the improvement of surviving native pinewoods in several significant schemes – within the confines of fencing – he had tried to direct the planting to the poorer areas. He was worried about using up perfectly good sitka spruce land for 'trees for the environment'.

'Forestry has changed in the last few years with the current native pinewood scheme. If you can get the economies of scale, the grant rate is quite attractive. It is more attractive at the moment than commercial forestry, although I worry that we are planting trees that will never be very good timber producers. We are planting trees for the environment, rather than as a crop. They must be regarded as a crop.'

Deerstalking is another major interest, with four lodges to rent, two of them currently tied up on a long lease, and there is a limited amount of pheasant-shooting. The sport guarantees a steady supply of shooters in the local hotels during the season, where the guests pad around in their woolly socks over teatime glasses of Scotch or gin, glad to be off the hill and rid of their boots, comparing the experiences of the day, the weather, the stalker, the difficulty of the stalk.

The stalking 'just about washes its face', said Gordon, while the pheasants make a loss.

The sport helps the local economy much more than the average hillwalker. The walker comes, goes out and walks for a day and brings his own lunch and drives home. The shooter will stay for a night or two, have a pretty high bar bill, and will go into the gun shop and stock up on cartridges or clothing.'

The history of deer hunting on Atholl goes back to the days of Queen Mary, when wolves were counted among the day's bag, though the serious interest in deerstalking dates from the end of the eighteenth century when the first purpose-built shooting lodge was created at Bruar. This illustrates a common misconception in modern reporting on Scotland's sporting tradition, which tends to tie the business to Queen Victoria and Albert and their creation of Balmoral. By 1800, in fact, the Atholl deer forest was let to a number of people including the Duke of Buccleuch.

Meanwhile, farming continues only because of the subsidies. Mrs Troughton has one farm and there are 20 farm tenants. The land is grassland, used for cattle and sheep. With sheep adding, in some areas, to the grazing pressure imposed by deer and rabbits.

'The worry is that unfenced ground is being over-utilised by grazing animals,' admitted Gordon. 'We are getting a large subsidy to keep sheep on hills that are being over-grazed. We could take the sheep off and receive a social subsidy – there is no other way of keeping people employed.'

Over-grazing, combined with some erosion, is evident in Glen Tilt itself, the central artery of the estate, where a few willows cling to unlikely rocks on the steep valley sides, and where the heather itself is being lost. Continuous heavy over-grazing can result in the heather being replaced by coarse grass. According to some environmentalists, the rate of erosion, and the loss of fertility on the hill, has increased in the past 20 years with the increase in sheep numbers on the land. There are instances of acute grazing on the limestone soils where the sheep tend to congregate.

And all of this on a major estate on the southern range of the Cairngorm Partnership area – the area arguably of greatest environmental potential, and concern, in upland Scotland. The area in which Scottish Natural Heritage is still trying to win concessions from landowners which would help regenerate the few surviving areas of native woodland.

Where does the fault lie? It is hard to say it is entirely the landowner's responsibility, and hard to say it is the tenant – who sees no other way of making a living than by increasing the number of sheep on the land. Both should realise, however, and the landowner in particular, that no other business in the world succeeds by eating into its capital – in this case the land itself. As long as sheep and deer are kept on the hills in unsustainable numbers, the capital will be eroded. It is happening very slowly – it will not be obvious in the lifetime of a keeper on that estate – but it is happening surely. And the signs are there for those who want to look. The problem may be that landowners and managers have accepted as natural the fact that there will be no natural regeneration without fencing to control the grazing animals.

For the tenants, there is the more pressing problem of the next rent review. Rents are set according to acreage and headage, and are reviewed every three years. Gordon carried out one review in 1993 and succeeded on that occasion in raising rents by an average of 27 per cent. It was the first review in nine years. 'It takes a long time, usually in the evening. You have a chat and everybody knows you are there to talk about the bloody rent and you are talking about everything except that! You probably don't mention the figure you are trying to get to for a while.

'The tenant naturally thinks it is too much. At the end of the day, you have a dram and shake hands or agree to come back. I haven't stuck with anybody yet. You must try to get on with the people you live next to.'

The estate employs around 70 people on a regular basis – it still operates one sawmill, and recently let one – and casual employment takes the figure to nearer 160 in the summer. This is a dramatic contrast with many big Highland estates which may employ no more than one or two stalkers over 50,000 acres. But still, said Gordon, it was not a viable unit.

'We are barely making enough money to cover our own running costs at the moment. We are selling the odd house, generating the odd bit of capital, just to stand still. The long-term future isn't terribly rosy.

'The estate had a large cash injection from the Cowdray family. Without income from outside, I don't think any Highland estate in Scotland would wash its face.'

The duke told me, in 1995, that if he had been asked as a boy in 1945 whether the large traditional estates would survive, he would have said no. But because they had survived for the past 50 years, he was no longer so sure.

'I think the big traditional estates probably can't survive, although I am not sure one is very good at seeing ahead.' He remained a stout defender of private land-ownership, but showed some sign of mellowing slightly by admitting that the acquisition by the National Trust of Mar Lodge estate might not be a bad thing; he was strongly opposed in the early 1990s to a proposed acquisition by environment groups.

Yet NTS ownership did slightly worry him, he said, because of the beliefs of some of its supporters. He believed the new regime on his neighbouring estate would mean a huge reduction in deer numbers in order to allow the Caledonian pine remnants to grow.

Here, the duke seemed to contradict himself. He agreed that a big reduction was needed, but 'not a reduction down to 10 per cent'. On Atholl land he accepted that 8,500 red deer were too many, and that the estate was affected by over-grazing. On the other hand, he said the task of getting numbers down and taking sheep off the high ground should be left to the private owners, and no reductions should be imposed on them. Thus espousing the good old familiar voluntary principle.

The duke's position – common among landowners – begged the question, how long can we wait for landowners to get the balance right?

'I believe there are too many deer and we are trying to reduce them. It is not always easy to reduce them because we believe in shooting in the season. I can't see it will do any good by having legislation which will force landowners to shoot a certain number of deer.' He said the estate would try to get numbers below 6,000. However, that figure was unlikely to lead to natural regeneration on the main chunk of Atholl land behind the castle.

His responsibilities as a landowner? 'I think, like every other landowner, I am always trying to improve the land, but it is not easy in Scotland because the land is not very good. The large landowners tend to be where the land is not much good. You don't get large landowners in East Lothian simply because the land is fertile and so much less is needed.

'I think that, so far, the public ownership that has come into Scotland has done a lot of good. But I don't want to get all of Scotland under public ownership. I think land should remain in private hands because, you know, too much land in public hands is a bore.'

It seemed, at least while the duke was around, that Atholl was under a microscope. When the Territorial Army helped out with flood damage on the Tilt, it was headline news in some papers. But it could have been argued that the estate could not afford to pay for such unforeseen work.

Almost every estate in Scotland, including the Queen's own Balmoral estate, accepts grants when they are available. I am very much in favour of giving a Perthshire estate hundreds of thousands of pounds if it will bring about an improvement in the landscape and environment which otherwise would not be achieved. As Atholl's last Scottish duke put it: 'One has got to take the grants when they are there.'

Educated at Eton, he graduated from Oxford with an MA degree and, at the age of 27, was elected to sit in the Lords. Estate employees had their own theories about the diffident bachelor duke and one remarked that his father died just at the point when he was to be sent to Eton, leaving a mark on the young George Iain Murray 'at a crucial point in his growing up'. He was aged 13 when he was told that his father had died while commanding the Scottish Horse.

At the time, Blair Castle – in common with many other stately homes – had been turned into a school for evacuees from Glasgow. The duke-to-be, in turn, had been evacuated from the castle to one of the shooting lodges, where he lived until his move to Eton.

His great interests were steeplechasing – he kept a couple of horses – and bridge, in which he led the House of Lords team. He was said to wear a black tie for dinner every night, even when dining alone, and he may be remembered, at least in part, for his revival of the Atholl Highlanders.

The 'private army' is, in fact, no more than a group of buddies who are given a free uniform and allowed to dress up for the odd ceremonial and touristic occasion. The right to retain an army was granted by Queen Victoria, who enjoyed the occasional visit to Blair Castle in the 1840s. Much earlier, a real Atholl army had been formed to fight in the American War of Independence. It apparently got as far as Portsmouth, by which time the war had ended.

If history was enough to sustain an estate, then Atholl would thrive. Like Lochiel estate to the west, it played a significant role in the '45. The first duke – created in 1703 – was Lord Privy Seal, a controversial figure who vociferously opposed the Act of Union. In what looks like an early rehearsal of the Scottish National Party argument of today, the duke wrote in March 1708 protesting that the shires and burghs royal within Scotland, which had 155 individual representatives, would have this number reduced in Parliament to 45, to be joined by 513 English representatives, 'where they can have no influence by reason of the vast disproportion of their numbers'. He was arrested for his troubles.

Going back further still, the visit of Queen Mary to the estate in 1564 is well documented. One account describes a great deer hunt arranged for the Queen in which 'two thousand Highlanders, or Wild Scotch as you call them here, were employed to drive all the deer from the wood and hills of Badenoch, Mar, Murray and other counties into one glen. Once in the glen they faced the Queen, the noblemen, and a large number of dogs. In the mayhem which followed, the Highlanders plunged spears and knives into the panic-stricken animals which were forced to break free of the encircling group.

'It was told the Queen that several of the Highlanders had been wounded and that two or three of them had been killed outright; and the whole body had got off, had not the Highlanders, by their skill in hunting, fallen upon a stratagem to cut off the rear from the main body. It was of those that had been separated that the Queen's dogs, and those of the nobility, made slaughter. There were killed that day 360 deer, with five wolves and some roes.' On the east side of Loch Loch – above Glen Tilt – is Tom nam Ban Righ, the Queen's Hillock, from where she is said to have viewed this sport.

The rich history is kept alive today by the impressive castle archives, which act as a useful resource for researchers.

In the view of Ron Greer, a resident of Blair Atholl and a campaigner for sustainable development in the Highlands, the estate might be damned with faint praise. 'They provide jobs but it is nothing like it could be, and should be. Nothing. People in Scottish cities accept the countryside as it is, because they do not realise there is an alternative. If only they realised they were being affected, they were being deprived of something. That you could create jobs for people in these places.'

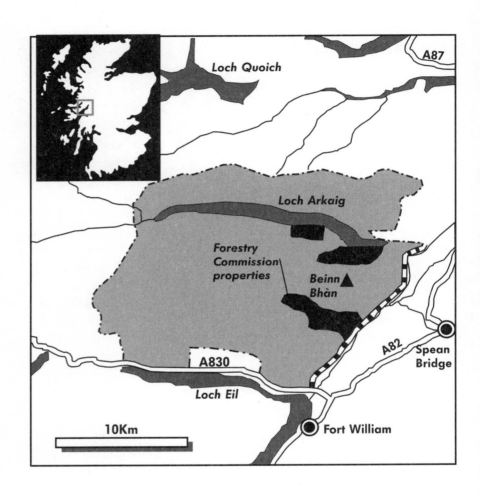

ACREAGE – 90,000
OWNER – CAMERON FAMILY, SIR DONALD CAMERON OF LOCHIEL
MANAGED FOR – SPORT, TOURISM, FORESTRY, FARMING LETS
POINTS OF INTEREST – JACOBITE HISTORY, OWNED BY SAME
FAMILY FOR 600 YEARS

CHAPTER SIX

Lochiel Estate

When *The Observer* asked eight clan chiefs to name the 'chiefs' chief', five of them chose Sir Donald Cameron of Lochiel, the twenty-sixth Lochiel to own the vast lands of moor and mountain west of Loch Lochy and the Great Glen. It is not hard to see why. This Lochiel –as they have all been known – is a sprightly octogenarian who is happy to expound his views on the clan, the land and the perils of private ownership. A highly successful businessman – former director of the Royal Bank of Scotland, chairman of the Scottish Railways Board, Crown Estate commissioner – he now lives in retirement in the compact square castle at Achnacarry, which sits perilously close to the fast River Arkaig. He rents the place from his eldest son, Donald Cameron, Younger of Lochiel, who works for a merchant bank in London.

The pleasing view from the front rooms takes in an expanse of paddock and the old beech trees which were being planted by his ancestor, the nineteenth Lochiel, on the very day in 1745 on which he heard that Bonnie Prince Charlie had landed in Scotland, and had called for his help.

Lochiel estate is remarkable for its family and for its Jacobite history. The present Lochiel is – without doubt – the sixteenth son, or brother, to own the land. His is often described as the twenty-sixth

Lochiel, but he points out that the first ten are unauthenticated. In his turn, he has made the land over to his own son. However the ownership is calculated, the fact remains that the same family has had the estate since the fourteenth century, when it was still based very firmly on the patriarchal clan system. A system finally dismantled – crushed rather – after Culloden.

The estate is also remarkable, as many of the old estates are, because the family has managed, through more than thin than thick, to hold on to the land. It once spanned 140,000 acres, and is today reduced to 90,000, 90 per cent of which is high moorland. There are just 170 acres of arable ground, it employs around ten people, and the average annual rainfall is 75 inches. 'Most of the land is of little value,' remarks the laird.

It has not been easy for Lochiel's ancestors to hold on. To an outsider, it barely makes sense. It has hardly ever made a useful profit, and at present does not look like it ever will. Yet, if it was sold today, it might fetch around £3 million to £4 million. Enough, you would think, to make the family rather comfortably well off. Even if life in a castle had to be forfeited.

This Lochiel has grasped the land to him with just as much tenacity as his forebears, and he remarks, with genuine feeling, that it was a close-run thing in the difficult 1920s when his father thought about selling up. He recalls his father going around the sporting agencies in London, hoping to find a rich sportsman to take the castle for deerstalking. At the time, the whole family would decant to Nairn, or to the nearby dower house at Clunes, while the richer people had their sport and the luxury of Achnacarry.

Lochiel, relaxed on the sofa in front of a two-bar electric fire, is in mustard cords, a grey herringbone tweed jacket, green cardigan, blue shirt and tie, and fine fettle. He is dapper, and thumps the spectacles he holds in his left hand on the arm of the chair to emphasise his views. As if keeping time to a country dance.

Outside the north widow is a fine view of the hill, swathed in plantation trees, and the swollen River Arkaig, which seems to threaten the garden fence, having been made big by melting snow on the tops. Lochiel is preoccupied with matters financial; he gives the impression that he has been for decades.

He admits the estate makes no money, and it therefore has no capital to reinvest in new businesses, or the 100-or-so tenants. If he wanted to assist a farmer by building a new shed to help him over-winter his sheep indoors, it would be difficult, because there would be no cash for the work. And it might not even be welcomed by the farmer, because his living is so marginal he would be unable to meet the increased rent.

Lochiel relates this state of affairs with a resigned joviality, as if it is all beyond the most enlightened management. His family has struggled to hold the ancestral home, but he remains convinced that private ownership is the best option. 'I think private land-ownership has proved over the years the best way of managing the land and helping the people who are on the land. If you have, like us, inherited with the land a knowledge of the countryside, a love of the countryside, a knowledge of the people who live on it, you have real interest in what is happening.

'You could argue, why should my family have it? I think it is a good way as any of making use of the land. But there is no doubt you get bad landowners, like you get bad anything. If you have nationalised land, who is going to run it? Are you going to put in managers who just get paid for what they do?'

Lochiel believes there is little scope for diversity, although he thinks it is necessary these days to broaden the economic base. He adds a note of caution, however, mentioning the example of the Lovat Frasers whose lands have been broken up by failed enterprise. (In fact, by the spendthrift actions of Simon Fraser, Master of Lovat, who died in 1994 leaving massive debts. Lochiel attended the funeral.)

To many critics, Lochiel's honest appraisal of the state of the family fortune and the lack of income from the land will serve to illustrate one of the problems of land-owning in Scotland. It is easy to use such examples as an argument for change – in the subsidy system, and in ownership itself. It is easy, even, to argue the land would be better owned by a rich businessman or foreign millionaire, rather than a venerable clan family.

The laird's impoverishment, of course, is not Everyman's. He enjoyed an impressive business career, is known worldwide as the chief of his clan and, in Achnacarry, has a delightfully appointed castle home. Though the decoration is wearing a little.

Economic realities for the Cameron family have meant the men going to London to make money. Sir Donald, now 87, was educated at Harrow and Balliol College, Oxford, and became a qualified chartered accountant. He served with the Lovat Scouts through the Second World War and later commanded the Queen's Own Cameron Highlanders (Territorials).

When he inherited the estate on his father's death in 1951, he returned to Scotland and was 'lucky enough' to be offered several part-time executive positions. These included, from 1954–80, a directorship of the Royal Bank of Scotland, and from 1957–59, the role of Crown Estate Commissioner. There were numerous other posts.

His two daughters and his eldest son were born in London, and his younger son was born in Inverness and educated at the local primary school before being sent south to private education (where it was remarked that he was well schooled in all the basics, but had been taught only Scottish history). His family spend holidays and spare time at the ancestral home.

In order to avoid death duties, he made over the estate to his son (land has to be made over seven years before the death of the owner to avoid duty), and he in turn has made over part of the property to his son. 'We haven't got tremendously valuable things in the house that we could readily sell. We had to take every possible precaution to make sure there weren't enormous death duties.' Thus, the passing of the lands from father to son is guaranteed for 18 indisputable generations, or 28, if the family portraits in Achnacarry are to be believed. On the wall of the drawing-room there are two family portraits by Raeburn, one of great-great-grandfather, one of great-great-grandmother.

Imagine Lochiel's amusement when *The Sunday Times*, in its annual magazine devoted to naming the richest people in Britain, included him in the list. 'We got on to them straightaway, and asked them to take us out the following year, which they did,' he chuckles. In the 1995 *Sunday Times* list, Sir Donald was absent. But can 90,000 acres really not make a living for one family?

The estate economy stands on the four legs of farming, deerstalking, forestry and tourism, with a welcoming leaning post in the form of salmon-farming on Loch Arkaig, where a fish-farming company rents several cages – 'and it costs the estate nothing'.

SHEEP

Sheep-farming has been a mainstay for centuries, and a drain on the land. In 1951, there were 10,000 sheep on the hills and the estate employed 12 shepherds. But it was an unprofitable time for sheep, according to the laird, and particularly so at the fank at Glen Dessary, at the west end of Loch Arkaig – 14 miles from the civilisation of Achnacarry. When the nearest school was closed the estate had to find single shepherds, or married men without children, to tend the remote sheep.

'We decided it wasn't on to have sheep so far away, so we took up a ranching system. The shepherds would stay here and would have to go out to their hirsels.' That system ended in 1960 when the sheep were taken off Glen Dessary and the flock was reduced to 6,000. When a second hirsel was sold on Loch Arkaig-side, the flock was down to 3,000, with four or five shepherds.

Now, the system has moved on again. The estate has opted for limited partnership farms in which farmers, including shepherds who had worked for the estate for years, pay a rent for the land and for the ewes. In return, they do all the work, get the subsidies, and any profit they can make. Which is little.

This development, however, is highly significant. 'It is generally quite popular. We have no shepherds at all, but it is undoubtedly beneficial,' says Lochiel. 'We get rent for land and ewes. Instead of making a big loss,' he thumps this out with the metronome of his left hand, 'we make a reasonable profit. They run their own farms and affairs, they don't make much money, but they make something out of it. They get the subsidies. It is nice for them.'

After centuries in which shepherds worked to make the estate a profit – if possible – the partnership does not amount to true emancipation. But it is enlightening enough that Lochiel admits the farmers and shepherds like to manage their own affairs. He did not use the word, but perhaps he was saying they like the sense of ownership.

The latest move came after the failure of a bold attempt to improve the profitability of sheep-farming. In the early 1970s, the estate sold the 20,000 acres of remote Glen Dessary as a deer forest with lodge. There were 'two or three extremely good offers', and the property was sold near the top of the international estate market. It has changed hands several times since and is now owned by a German called Schmidt, a wealthy furniture-maker who visits every year for the deerstalking. 'He has even put in a hydro-electric scheme and installed electricity in the house,' remarks Lochiel. 'He has improved it a lot.'

The money helped buy Lochiel's heir a house in London, and allowed the estate to buy a farm, outside Clackmannan in central Scotland, which would be used to over-winter sheep. The idea was that the animals would be taken to the farm to be fattened. Gradually, the Clackmannan farm became unprofitable and it has now been sold – 'we thought we might make a fortune out of it, but we didn't'. After many readjustments, Lochiel declares himself happy with the first leg of his economy.

RED DEER

Another leg is provided by the age-old sport of stalking. Stalking, remarks Lochiel, is no longer profitable.

'It has to be done, it is fun, and it is something I would hate to lose. One day it might be profitable. We sell the venison and the price has been up to 90p per pound, and down to 50p.' At the top rate, a stag will be worth £200 to the estate, on top of the £200 which the stalking client will be asked to pay for his kill. If he is staying for a week, and has a stag a day, his bill for the shooting alone will be £1,000. The estate shoots 140 stags a year, and the beasts have a current capital value of around £15,000 each.

Back in the 1920s depression, Lochiel's father relied on the income from stalking. 'In the 1920s my father found it very difficult. Sheep were very poor and he depended on letting the deerstalking with the house. I can remember going round visiting agents in London to see if we could get anyone interested.

'We used to take a small house in Nairn and live there for the stalking seasons. The tenants would have Achnacarry for all of August and September. At that time it was done purely for the pleasure of stalking, but after the war the venison became quite valuable.

'We let the estate to the Savoy Hotel in London who took it for the meat. They got all the venison for three or four years, but when the meat rationing stopped, they stopped dead. They hadn't established a taste for the meat, and we had to go back to the old game of letting.'

There are three separate deer forests for let, Achdalieu, Achnacarry South and Achnacarry North, stretching between Loch Eil in the south and Glen Kingie in the north, with the River Lochy and the Caledonian Canal roughly marking the eastern boundary. Although Lochiel no longer vacates his castle to the shooters, the dower house of Clunes, not far from Achnacarry, is available. Those looking for cheaper sport stay in the local hotels or B&Bs. 'Stalking is not now paying, and that is true of any big forests in the Highlands.'

TOURISM

This third support is little more substantial than the rest. The estate used to let a number of cottages, but found the business of cleaning up between customers 'a bit of a nuisance'. Now it has longer lets for about 12 properties, a cottage on Loch Arkaig taken on a weekly basis by fishermen, and the estate's staff inhabit five or six other houses. The clan itself is a major part of the tourist attraction.

Every five years, Achnacarry hosts a clan gathering. At the event of 1956, Lochiel recalled that his father, 18 years earlier, had talked about the land being put into a clan trust for perpetuity. He told the assembled Camerons that if economic pressures ever made it impossible for the family to hold on, then he would ask the clan to consider the same proposal again, before turning to the open market.

Since then, with the help of an appeal for funds to friends and clan members around the world, Lochiel and his son have raised £50,000 with which to restore and rebuild an old cottage which dates from the time of the '45, and which now acts as the clan museum. (It serves an additional function, during its opening months from April to October, in that it reduces the number of root-seeking Camerons from the Antipodes knocking on the front door of Achnacarry to hail the chief.)

The museum, which attracts 7,000 visitors annually, is a small but impressive affair, telling neatly, without over-elaboration, a little bit about the estate, and majoring, not surprisingly, on Prince Charles Edward Stuart and his exploits with the Gentle Lochiel. For his troubles, Lochiel's ancestor had to flee to France while Cumberland's troops burnt down the old, wooden-built Achnacarry Castle.

The museum sticks mainly to the romantic, not bothering to disillusion visitors with the truth about the Young Pretender who lied to the clan chiefs over the support he expected to receive from his friends in France, and showed himself at Culloden to be a disastrous military leader, despite the undoubted abilities of his clan armies, which marched further into England than any other Scottish army.

Outside the museum is an old cannon and a picnic bench. Above the building are some mixed native broad-leaves and, further up the hill, some surviving Scots pine, looking like their seed has no future. On the cold January day of my visit, there were a dozen or more young stags grazing near the low building, as tame as the estate dogs. They watched us as we pulled up in the car and did not bother to move off when we got out.

Deer are strikingly attractive animals and seeing them so close against the backdrop of the Achnacarry parklands, with the sun nearly gone down on a winter afternoon, was a thrill, even if they were present for a questionable reason. The animals were there for the winter feed which the keepers put out for them every afternoon. Feeding stags helps them through the season and helps to keep them – they are stravaiging animals – on the estate and out of any nearby turnip patches (and, most probably, the farmer's freezer). But you might also conclude it is proof that the land itself does not have enough to offer them in such numbers.

FORESTRY

The estate has planted around 1,000 acres of sitka – 'nowadays you have to be very environmentally minded and put in birch and God knows what all' – and it has sold around 15,000 acres of land to the Forestry Commission.

Thinnings are taken after 15 years and the wood is clear-felled at 40 to 50 years, following normal practice for commercial species. Lochiel used to be able to sell wood to the pulp mill at Fort William, which finally went the way of many doomed Highland enterprises.

He is a supporter of 1950s and '60s-style commercial forestry, although the estate has one pinewood regeneration scheme on the side of Loch Arkaig, and he remarks that there are some 'quite good Scots fir' at the far end of the loch. There was a surviving stand of Scots pine by the side of the loch – although there was no natural regeneration – until the last war when it was burnt down in a fire started accidentally by the Commandos who used Achnacarry as their main training centre.

Loch Arkaig is also home to the ghosts of the crofting community cleared by Donald Cameron of Clunes, in 1801. Six families spent the night in the graveyard above Clunes, watching their houses burn down.

'It wasn't as bad here as in some other parts,' notes Lochiel. 'Although we did clear a lot of tenants off the sides of Loch Arkaig. There were an enormous number. It must have been a very low standard of living, which couldn't have gone on.

'One paid a bit for it. Some of them got help to move abroad. Some were moved to the great glen and got jobs working on the canal. If you did it today they would have said "what a marvellous thing to do". The land went to big sheep-farmers. There is no one there now. The crofters used to take their cattle up to the hills, and when the potatoes came, they grew potatoes. They had their ceilidhs and their singing.'

This justification, that the standard of living must have been bad, is common throughout the Highlands, and was used by factors from Sutherland to South Uist to justify the removal of those people who once enjoyed a close allegiance with their clan chief and showed great loyalty to him. The museum does not record the fact – although it hints as much – that the actions of the early nineteenth-century Lochiel would have been unthinkable to his ancestors 100 years before. One eighteenth-century Lochiel became famous for biting out the throat of an English soldier – based at the nearby garrison of Fort William – who had pinned him to the ground.

Dr James Hunter, in his book *Scottish Highlanders, A People and Their Place*, skilfully chronicles the sea-change which saw the Gaelic-speaking can chiefs renounce their ancient tongue and take up the ways and the values of the English government, so that, within a century, chiefs who had enjoyed a symbiotic relationship with their folk were moved to clear the same people from the land in brutal evictions.

Some campaigners argue today that the education of the present Lochiel and his family in southern public schools and universities, and of other landowners like him, is the modern expression of the distancing of the laird from his land and its people.

'On this estate today, we have quite a lot of crofters who have security of tenure. They pay a comparatively small rent. Sometimes they can be a nuisance. In the old days you might help them in various ways, sometimes by giving them timber to build a fence.' A number of crofters have bought their land from Lochiel (a little bit of hard cash for the estate), and around 100 tenants remain, rearing their sheep for meat. The animals are gathered in June from the high ground and the lambs are sold on as stores.

'The crofters do quite well, they get a lot of grants from the Crofters' Commission, they get grants for building houses. If they sell a bit of land for development within five years of taking over the croft, they have to give half to the landowner, but if they sell it after five years, they get it all.'

Remote though it is, Lochiel estate is not immune to the vagaries of Euro legislation. The landowner is exercised by the regulations which have raised the standards required in the estate larder, where the deer are butchered, ready for collection by the game dealer. 'I suppose it is a good thing, but the cost of getting a good deer larder that passes all the Euro-conditions is out of this world.' He is also subject to the recent laws on drinking-water quality: '. . . at certain temperatures you can have too many bacilli, so you have to put in a filter thing which is going to cost over £500 per house. That sort of thing suddenly falls on one. It really does rather floor one. For as long as I know, we have been drinking perfectly happily from the stream.'

Perhaps as much as any economic consideration, the estate is kept alive today by its proud Jacobite history. Previous Lochiels supported Robert the Bruce, Queen Mary and fought at Killiecrankie. The entrance of Achnacarry is hung with swords and other memorabilia commemorating the mythologised campaign of Prince Charlie.

The Lochiel of 1745 was said to be far sighted, ahead of his time. He was known as the Gentle Lochiel because he tried to make peace with the neighbouring clans and worked to improve his land. He was in the act of planting beech trees when the word came that the prince had landed, with just seven men, and had summoned his most loyal chief to his side. The escapade, although it included remarkable victories, was ill-timed because it came at a period when it did not suit the interests of France to support a Stuart uprising in Britain.

Lochiel was said to be disappointed by the news of the arrival, but felt an obligation to meet his prince. He was determined he would turn him back to France. 'The latest theory,' observes the latest Lochiel, 'is that he was not won over by the Prince's charm, but by the plea, "If you don't bring your men, what will happen to me?".'

Lochiel returned to Achnacarry to call out his men, and other Jacobite estates followed suit – as the Prince knew they would. The standard was raised at Glenfinnan on 19 August and the rest is history. It ended with Lochiel, who was wounded in both ankles at Culloden, fleeing to France with the Prince. During the well-documented flight, the Prince spent several nights in the vicinity of Achnacarry – probably between 15 and 22 August 1746 – at a time when there was a £32,000 reward for information leading to his capture.

Behind the fleeing Pretender came the Duke of Cumberland's soldiers. They burnt the houses of Achnacarry and the old castle, which had been made of Scots pine planks in 1660. The Government's intention was to smash the clan system so that never again would chiefs raise armies against the Crown. It worked.

Crops were destroyed, land was forfeited to the Crown, and Acts were passed making it illegal to wear the kilt, carry arms or play the pipes. The Jacobite leaders had to flee, or face banishment or imprisonment. One of them, the head of the Lovat Frasers, was the last person to be beheaded in Britain. His descendants soon switched allegiance to the King.

It was not until the General Act of Indemnity in 1784 that Donald Cameron, 23rd chief, was able to buy back the Lochiel lands for £3,433 9s 1d. But this Lochiel had been brought up in France and England, and had little knowledge of the clan system or dependency. The museum records state: 'The Lochiel who went into exile was the father and protector of his people, the one who returned was a landlord.' Had it been the same ever since?

Lochiel appears to be a popular laird, although some observers believe his family today is simply presiding over the ongoing demise of the estate – a view not shared by Lochiel and his sons.

The primary school at Achnacarry closed in 1995, in part as a result of the reduction in employment on the estate. Councillor Dr Michael Foxley complains that while his own south side of Loch Eil has a reasonably healthy population of crofters, the north shore on Lochiel estate is virtually barren, the crofts long gone.

The Lochiel story is one of the enduring nature of some of Scotland's oldest clans, and the family today, as it has always done, continues to enjoy establishment connections at the highest level.

In 1974, Lochiel was made a Knight of the Thistle by the Queen at

St Giles Cathedral and, in the same good year for the family, Donald Cameron, Younger of Lochiel, was married to Lady Cecil Kerr, daughter of the Marquis and Marchioness of Lothian. The ceremony involved both Cardinal Gordon Gray, Archbishop of St Andrews and Edinburgh, and a former Moderator of the General Assembly of the Church of Scotland. The bride wore the Cameron family tiara and the bridegroom wore a blue velvet jacket once worn by his great-grandfather.

One of the 800 guests was the Prince of Wales, who today bears the title Lord of the Isles. The title is honorary, meaningless, but for several hundred years the Lordship held sway in the Western Highlands and Islands and Gaelic culture flourished and spread.

That was quite another place.

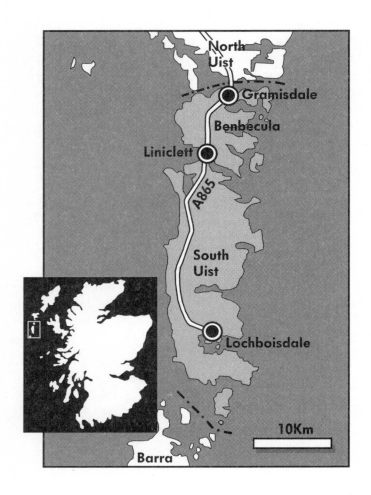

ACREAGE – 90,000+
OWNER – SYNDICATE OF NINE FAMILIES
MANAGED FOR – SPORT
POINTS OF INTEREST – BIGGEST CROFTING ESTATE, FAMED FOR
TROUT-FISHING, SNIPE-SHOOTING

CHAPTER SEVEN

South Uist Estate

(*Including Benbecula and Eriskay*)

If you are used to the Hebridean holiday islands, Colonsay for example, or Rum or even Coll, then the Uists are bound to be a visual disappointment. Particularly South Uist.

I arrived on the Caledonian MacBrayne ferry from Skye, having left behind the attractive village of Uig, which just about conforms with the picture-postcard image, for the scruffy practicality of Lochmaddy and the Western Isles.

There is a lesson to be learned for those who tour the Highlands and Islands looking for the mind's-eye image around every bend, at the top of every rise in the thin road rolling through the peatlands. Much of what is valued scenically as the character of the Highlands is lacking in people; cleared of people.

We don't mind the odd attractive cottage or mansion here and there, perhaps at the head of a sea loch or perched on a headland in the spit of the Atlantic, but we do not want the higgledy-piggledy crofting township with its abandoned tractors, real and toy, its half-ruined crofts and its half-finished bungalows, the unattractive harling and the sheep and their shit getting everywhere underfoot.

Some townships, of course, are worse than others. And because those of us not from the crofting communities have learned sympathy for the crofter over the years, it seems almost rude to find the houses on the machair ill-fitting and ugly, to wonder why these Hebridean sons of Somerled don't bother to clear up the mess. There are many reasons. It may be the fact that crofters are crofters only after 5 p.m. and on Saturdays, and therefore only have time for the black faces which, by and large, manage to look after, and die (quite easily), themselves. It may be that they are unemployed, lacking in motivation, lacking in facilities and the support which would improve their lives. And it may be that many of the best people from the community have always, and still do, leave the islands. That some of those left – and we have to be allowed to think this – may be lazy or ignorant, or both. That the great spirit of warm humanity and generosity redolent of the pacific crofter may not, after all, apply to every man on his croft. Crofters may be no different from the rest of us.

It is as well to get these thoughts out of the way early on during a visit to a place such as South Uist, as romantic notions are wont to return. Gloomy contemplations come easier in dull weather when the lochs are a lead-grey cloth, the machair is flat and uninteresting and the hills on the east coast have a beaten, sheep-chewed look about them.

The feeling is unlikely to last. Scotland is famous for its sudden changes in weather, the Western Isles more so than any other part. The scenery can change as quickly as pictures on a film reel: blue sky and sunshine blowing in from the broad Atlantic to drop a blanket of May greenness on the machair. Suddenly, the lochs are blue, the swans brilliant white, the fields impossibly green and the occasional blue or red-roofed croft is like a water painting against a vast sky. The township that was scruffy becomes quaint, almost natural. The crofter that was lazy, commendably laid-back. All that is required to complete the picture is to meet the natives themselves, the majority of whom – on south Uist, at least – are welcoming and open.

And in those cloudy intervals where you are lamenting the grim council houses just south of the causeway from Benbecula (and the generally appalling standard of rural housing throughout Scotland), bear in mind that your hire car was left at the pier at Lochmaddy with the keys in an envelope and a request that you top up the tank and leave the appropriate money in the unlocked vehicle when you depart. The telephone booking was taken without an address, just a surname. Cars are not locked, crime is negligible, violence rare.

The finer points of the place and the people are not necessarily visible in the scenery, as you initially expect them to be. Many casual observers link the easy-going, laissez-faire attitude of the islanders with the Catholic religion which holds sway in the place, and contrast the welcome to be found on Barra and South Uist with that found, say, on the staunchly Free Church island of Harris. It was a North Uist man – a Protestant himself – who first propounded this theory to me. He also claimed that while enterprise flourished on Barra, it was long since dead on dour Harris.

These conflicting images of the Western Isles, scenic and social, are all part of the attraction for those who live there, and particularly for those who move there from other parts of Britain. They may also be part of the attraction for those who live and work in London and look to Scotland for a slice of sanity and peace. And perhaps fishing and shooting.

South Uist estate is the biggest island estate in Scotland, it includes virtually all of Benbecula, South Uist and Eriskay, with the exception of some land owned by Scottish Natural Heritage at the Druidibeg National Nature Reserve, and 15,000 acres compulsorily purchased by the military for the rocket range and training grounds on Benbecula and South Uist.

It covers more than 90,000 acres and since the early 1960s has been owned by a largely English syndicate (there are three Scottish members) which uses the island and its old lodge for sport, principally the renowned sea-trout fishing and the sporting delicacy of snipe-shooting.

Any fly-fisherman will understand the attraction of the place immediately. The machair lochs hold large trout which are not easily tempted, but which will make the reel scream when they take under the permanently rippled surface. And while the fish are not rising, the fisherman will be cocooned in the sounds of the machair, the plaintive curlew, the insisting lapwing and the staccato redshank; swans will creak past on slow-motion wings and the hum of the Atlantic will hang in the wind.

Like an old landed family, the men who set up the syndicate on South Uist are passing on the property and a love of the place to their sons – merchant bankers, wine merchants and the like.

The island was bought in 1962 for the now remarkable sum of £60,000 – around £7,000 per syndicate member, or the price of a decent house at the time. The men who were attracted to South Uist were keen fishermen based in Ayrshire, the Glasgow stockbroker David Greig and his friend, Adam Hamilton. Having visited the island and realised what could be had for the price – the purchase figure included the shooting lodge and almost all the fishing rights – the pair contacted friends and family and the money was found. A few years later, they bought the Lochboisdale Hotel for another £60,000.

In the mid-1990s, David Ruck Keene, a merchant banker with SBC Warburg in the City, and Rupert Ponsonby, a London-based wine importer, took control of the company, which is incorporated and has had shareholders since 1970.

Each year the families agree which weeks they will take, between mid-July and September, in Grogarry Lodge. It is available for let at other times.

Most of the syndicate members, who are now running into the problem of expanding family members and increasing demand, are fishermen and women, but their interests, reflecting modern concerns and attitudes, have developed over the years to include some of the many non-sporting attractions. These might involve the history of the old Clanranald chiefs, the beaches and hills, corncrakes, Flora MacDonald, Compton Mackenzie's *Whisky Galore* (set on Eriskay), and Prince Charles Edward Stuart, one-time fugitive of this place.

It is quite easy to surmise, when the sun suddenly spreads over the machair in mid-May and the skylark has returned from Africa to warble its summer song, when the irises are not quite high enough for the corncrake, but the first of the myriad wildflowers are appearing from the shell-sand soil, that all is well in the great scheme of things. That life is not so bad after all, even in the super-heated South.

The estate just about manages to make a profit, largely on the basis that the syndicate members are rich enough to pay the going rate for their own fishing trips; none of the directors takes money out of the company. There is enough left over to pay seven full-time staff, including two joiners, two gamekeepers and a resident factor, and to carry out some basic improvements on the ground, directed, of course, mainly towards the sporting interest.

The 1993 company accounts reveal a profit before tax almost doubling from 1992 to £76,337, around £70,000 of which was due to the sale of assets. The annual report suggests that profits and land and asset sales are likely to range between £10,000 and £20,000 a year, as long as there are assets to dispose of.

David Ruck Keene, over beer and sandwiches in the Great Northern Hotel next to King's Cross Station, reveals strong feelings for the island. The guiding priorities are to run the place commercially and harmoniously.

This last objective is the most difficult, requiring as it does a level of support and co-operation from over 900 crofters. Many landowners and agents would not envy the syndicate such a large crofting interest. An Edinburgh chartered surveyor once confessed to me after a lengthy discourse on dealing with crofters; 'You may gather, off the record, that I do not like crofters. They are quite impossible to deal with. They receive enormous subsidies, a level of support which applies nowhere else – it did not apply to the miners when they lost their jobs and it does not apply to anybody in the city – but they get the money and they still complain, and they do their best to make life difficult for the landowner.' A common enough view in such company.

By and large, the syndicate appears to be well regarded by a majority of the crofters, although Ruck Keene suggests there are one or two 'troublemakers'. He adds that the syndicate members are far removed from the kind of incidents he has heard of in both Lewis and Harris, where absentee landowners have had their cars spat on by locals.

He sees certain advantages in ownership by a syndicate, suggesting that a single laird is likely to have a limited range of interests in the property, perhaps confined only to sport. The syndicate, he says, brings a lot of people to the islands – five families now have their own houses on South Uist – and it guarantees some local employment. Locals, he adds, are specifically consulted on some issues.

Here, as elsewhere, the sporting possibilities provided by a degraded landscape dominate management policy. The fishing was run, until recently, 'by the seat of the pants', according to Ruck Keene, but is now being developed with the longer term in mind, and with the help of a Glasgow-based hydro-engineer who specialises in fishing-waters.

His recommendations have confirmed the value of the practice of gravel being flown from the shore by helicopter to replenish spawning redds for the precious sea trout and salmon. Some redds have been lost to silt washed off the peat in heavy rains, others have been removed by flooding – both indications of the need for man to manage an unnatural environment if it is to produce a healthy crop.

John Kennedy, the fishing manager on the island, formerly an army sergeant, points out that the sea trout run is still healthy in this furthest reach of the Hebrides, in contrast to the fortunes of the mainland game fishery in Loch Maree and other parts of the north-west mainland. He attributes this, in part, to the fact that there are no salmon-farming enterprises on the west coast of South Uist; elsewhere, particularly in Ireland, many people are convinced that salmon farms, and the parasitical sea lice which thrive in them, are an important cause of the decline in sea trout numbers.

In the early 1980s, the annual sea trout catch on the estate dipped, but in 1995 there was a healthy total of 383 fish landed – excluding all those under a pound and a half, which must be returned.

Not surprisingly, the recommendations for improving the fishing include the planting of broad-leaved trees along river edges and around lochs to help ameliorate the acidity coming off the peaty hills, and to provide important insect life and nutrients for fish and other organisms in the water. Such planting, although known to be important, is extremely rare in Scotland, suggesting a dearth of environmental and biological knowledge among those who manage vast estates. Unfortunately, there are enough sheep on the open hill – although the majority are kept on low ground – and enough deer to prevent any natural regeneration. So the planting will only succeed if accompanied by fencing.

On the east side of the island, by Loch Eynort, Scottish Natural Heritage is involved in a regeneration experiment in which part of the hillside exhibiting remnant woodland – some of the island lochs also contain shrubs and small trees – has been fenced from deer. Regeneration is continuing apace, showing that, in terms of potential, the bare hills on the outer isles are not much different from the treeless landscapes of the mainland. The estate has an interest in this particular project because the trees will provide useful habitat for woodcock, another popular target for visiting guns. A number of the same birds may also die by flying into the fences at dawn and dusk.

There are other efforts which help maintain biodiversity, and support sport. There is a nature reserve at Loch Druidibeg, a convenient parcel of land set up in 1957, when, no doubt, it was also recognised by the owner as one of the less important stretches of water. It is a large, shallow, nutrient-poor loch dotted with islands, with some surviving wood scrub, but it is also one of the best examples in Britain of the gradual change from inland acid moorland in the east to western coastal grasslands, or machair.

Ruck Keene likes to think of Druidibeg as a useful sanctuary and breeding ground for wildlife. While the surrounding terrain has been affected by centuries of fires and grazing, its islands contain nature's own woody sculptures – wind-pruned willow, rowan and birch above juniper, primrose, wild hyacinth, angelica and meadowsweet. The loch is a breeding ground for one of Britain's few resident populations of greylag geese, and it offers safe nesting to mute swan, heron, red- and black-throated diver and merganser. Birds of prey include the golden eagle, hen harrier, peregrine and merlin.

Elsewhere, there are calcium-rich machair lochs which teem with much greater life and are designated as Sites of Special Scientific Interest in their own right.

According to the owners, both sport and conservation share in the benefits wrought from the control of predators, principally crows and black-backed gulls. The hooded crow has almost been wiped out on the island, and as a result there has been a notable increase in the young of many species. The snipe-shooting – offering one of the toughest challenges in the sporting calendar – is said to be second to none. In 1995, 1,500 birds were shot on South Uist – without complaint from the conservation agency.

Of course, the occasions on which sport and conservation genuinely go hand in hand are only likely to occur where there is a useful spin-off for the dominating interest of the landowner, rather than the conservationist. South Uist, for all its painterly beauty and clean Atlantic beaches, remains a very much altered island, with no incentives available at the moment to improve the health of the hills on a wider scale.

SNH and the crofters, for example, share a concern with the reintroduction of red deer in the 1970s. Although the animal was an island native, its passing was hardly missed in the already over-grazed landscape and its return has resulted in conflict. The same crofters are concerned about the 1,200 resident geese, and would like to see many more shot in order to protect the 'early bite' they want for their sheep in springtime and, in the autumn, the crops being grown for winter fodder.

There is a committee which seeks agreement on the management of geese, but the estate seems, at present, to have no firm plan for the 200 or so red deer which it considers a small number for the size of the island. Red deer, of course, can multiply dramatically in the right conditions.

Driving through South Uist is an odd affair. The A865 – in better nick than the road from Lochmaddy on North Uist, which sets out across the peatlands like Atlantic breakers rolling underneath a small boat – roughly splits the centre of the island where the acid moor and mountain terrain of the east meets the naturally lime-rich shell sand of the machair. Machair is produced by the prevailing winds blowing the sand over the underlying Lewisian gneiss. The resultant habitat is both highly attractive and rare in world terms.

Machair and the traditional crofting carried out on it are vital for one of Britain's rarest birds, the corncrake. The distinctive shy creature, which annually completes a remarkable migration between South Africa and South Uist, only to then hide and skulk in the irises and the grass, has been wiped out in most of Scotland by modern farming techniques which allowed the earlier cropping of hay. On the Uists and Coll and Tiree, innovative schemes which give financial support to crofters have resulted in later harvesting and the survival of a few key populations.

Yet in South Uist all the concerted efforts by the Royal Society for the Protection of Birds, and the designation of the island as part of an Environmentally Sensitive Area – which qualifies it for corncrake-saving European money – have not assured the future of the birds. In 1995 there were 49 calling males on South Uist, in 1993 there were 50 and back in 1978 there were 83.

The drop is not a reflection of conservation effort, but of the fact that the crofting population of South Uist is ageing and becoming less inclined to practise traditional haymaking. If hay or silage is not grown, then the birds are confined to the plentiful irises and, later, to the machair.

The success of the corncrake is strictly bound up with a flourishing crofting scene, and the decline of that way of life will harm the bird, despite the best efforts of the RSPB. For the moment, its rasping call is still common enough in Uist, unheard throughout the Scottish mainland.

Crofting is often portrayed, particularly these days by the crofters and their leaders, as a very environmentally positive form of management of the land, and traditional crofting methods – where still maintained – are certainly beneficial. The habit of letting livestock graze on the machair in winter and on the higher land in the summer has done much to preserve the character of the flower-rich meadows.

On this estate, almost more than any other, the relationship with the crofters is important. Neal MacMillan, a crofter at Milton whose grandfather was cleared in the nineteenth century by the notorious Col. Gordon of Cluny, remarked that the syndicate had been a good owner, and that any problems have been caused by successive estate factors.

In the mid-1990s, the estate appointed Tim Atkinson, who formerly worked on Exmoor. The previous incumbent left after the police found him carrying a loaded pistol in his car; it was an incident which was unusually disturbing in a place like South Uist, where the need for personal protection is rarely a matter of debate.

There have been a few factors over the years who have not made the grade, and who have failed to understand crofting law, according to MacMillan. He named Peter Voy, now factor at Assynt estate, as an exception. During my own visit, in Atkinson's first few weeks on the island, the new man was making an effort to meet the people and to visit every corner. A book on Crofting Law was prominent on his desk in the estate office at Askernish, a fact which made MacMillan smile.

'He will have to know that,' he remarked. 'Some people come in here with the wrong ideas. They think they can push the crofters around, but they are wrong about that.' This assertion is evident in a number of Gaelic sayings which have been recorded locally on the subject of 'the estate', *an oighreachd*. For example, 'when a factor comes, he brings a new law with him', and the caution, 'slippery is the threshold of the big house'.

While they might not understand the local language, the syndicate and the factor enjoy one advantage in modern management of the land, and that is the simple fact that they do not carry with them the baggage of the Clearances – unlike the Sutherland family of today – which were particularly brutal on South Uist.

Here, as in Sutherland, the Clearances remain topical. The resolution of the original crime is within living memory for many of the older crofters. It was as late as the 1920s that some of the large sheep farms created by the former owner – Gordon of Cluny – were broken up, following more than 15 years of land raids and unrest and divided crofts.

MacMillan's farm at Milton was vacated by his grandfather as a boy in the nineteenth century at the behest of the absentee laird and his unpopular factor, Duncan Shaw. This was the same factor who, in the first decade of the nineteenth century, did his best to ensure that emigration did not happen because the landlord needed the people to collect tangles and bladder wrack to turn into the kelp used in the making of soap and glass in the south. There was a huge profit to be made from kelp. The income for the island's clan chief, Clanranald, was said to be over £9,400 in 1807, compared to income from the land rent of £5,300.

When the kelp prices finally collapsed in the late 1820s, it was the same Shaw who decided the only solution was to ship thousands of people out of South Uist and to convert to sheep farms. Accordingly, the townships were cleared throughout the 1820s and 1840s, sometimes with the help of police from Glasgow, and people were herded like baying cattle on to boats. 'If you didn't get out,' said MacMillan, 'your thatch went up.' When his grandfather was cleared in 1841, Frobost was home to 70 people, ten years later it was home to 12. His grandfather was one of those who did not leave the island, moving instead to the poorer ground of Daliburgh. The same thing was going on up and down the western islands and throughout the west Highlands. In many cases, the people here, and in Harris, were cleared from the relatively fertile machair lands in the west to the barren, acid, rocky lands of the east. It is still a wonder today that people could ever eke a crop from the lunar landscape of east Harris.

As recently as 1939, according to MacMillan, it was just about possible to make a full-time living at crofting. 'Crofting was the only living here at that point, and it was, more or less, an existence. People didn't go hungry but they didn't have all the comforts they have today. Then work and wages came to the island and everybody wants a weekly wage.'

No one expects a living from the croft today and the business is inevitably dominated by sheep, which, as the crofter and ghillie Neilly Johnstone comments, is not good for the land. When he helped his father on a Daliburgh croft in the 1940s, only two of the 23 crofts were without cattle, today only three have cattle.

Crofting is, however, supported by a generous grants system which provides up to £29,000 towards the cost of building a house. The grants system is a worthy and necessary tool in keeping people in the remote areas and sustaining a way of life which is both socially and culturally beneficial, and relatively easy on the land. But there are still not enough jobs outside the croft to make these communities particularly stable, or young.

The extreme poverty of the past has gone, although, as recently as 1972, a survey of housing in the Western Isles showed that 58 per cent of homes on South Uist were substandard, and 74 per cent on Barra.

As Dr Jim Hunter pointed out in *The Making of the Crofting Community*, the crofting story has come full circle from the period of congestion and land hunger in the late nineteenth century – the first raid in which crofters claimed back their land was on Skye in 1881 – to the late twentieth century and depopulation and the departure of young people. A comment from the Crofters Commission best sums up the value of the current system, albeit not a perfect one. It says, simply, that crofting is a way of life which should not be judged in terms of profit and loss.

Crofting does actually keep people on the land. On Mull, where the crofts were amalgamated into farms on the basis that this was more economically sensible, the result has been depopulation.

Crofting has a way to go. The current reliance on sheep is unhealthy, and there is a reluctance among crofters to purchase their property, as they are entitled to do for just 15 times the annual rental. As owners, they would lose access to a wide range of grants after a period of seven years. (On the other hand, the view of the Assynt crofters is that there are alternative development grants and opportunities open to landowners which are never open to crofters – for example, control of forestry, water and mineral rights.)

David Ruck Keene believes Assynt was the catalyst for the current land debate. 'Should land be owned by absentee landowners who have very little knowledge of the people who live there, and who go there to shoot twice a year?' He believes it should.

Community ownership, he suggests, can create problems over who benefits from the sporting income and how it is divided up. And he doubts that a community trust would manage the sporting asset as well as the sporting landowner. He also sees a problem in raising money to buy the land in the first place and does not expect community ownership to spread.

'Personally, I think it is a very appealing idea in theory, but in practice it is very unlikely.' In South Uist he would like to see the estate become more involved with the local community, in a 'low-profile' fashion, with the community coming to the syndicate with ideas.

For the non-sporting visitor, one of the most striking failures in the place is the lack of attention accorded to noteworthy historical monuments, quite apart from the fast-declining ruins of old thatched crofts, the turf still green on many of them and the thin timbers showing through. Flora MacDonald's birthplace, a collapsing croft, sits behind a modern croft and is marked only by a cairn. There is no path to it and the historically curious are obliged to walk up a crofter's drive and climb his fence to get to the place.

The ancient college and monastery remains at Howmore Church are overgrown, rundown and fast disappearing. This was a place of great importance to Gaelic antiquity, and the burial place of many Clanranald chiefs, but it is without a single sign, board, or interpretation of any kind. Is this quaint simplicity, or a shocking disregard of important remains? Or is the demand for such care and attention just the judgement of visitors applying their own modern standards?

Such sites, I believe, should be protected and cared for. When I asked Ruck Keene if the estate had a role to play, he replied that there was no legal obligation to maintain historical monuments, but thought the estate would be 'prepared to contribute to such a thing', especially if the approach was made by the local community. 'We are not interested in imposing our own values, and driving anything forward ourselves.'

History, meanwhile, is disappearing everywhere beneath the grass in a process of natural burial. There are the chambered cairns of the New Stone Age farmers and herdsmen of Neolithic times, dating from 6,000 years ago. There are wonderful standing stones from between 1000 and 2000 BC, and the remains of Iron Age (600 BC to AD 500) brochs and duns scattered throughout the Uists and the Western Isles. One of those distinctive roundhouses is visible on a tiny islet in the machair loch of Upper Loch Bornish.

The colourful life story of the place should be fascinating to the visitor, yet is explained here no more than in most of the Western Isles where tourism is regarded as an admission of failure and interpretive facilities are sadly lacking.

Consider, for example, the much-lamented story of the Lordship of the Isles. Christianity was brought by Columba to Iona and the Isles, and gave way to a lengthy period of Norse domination, which ended, in turn, with the creation of the much-lamented Lordship of the Isles (a title enjoyed today by the Prince of Wales).

The Lordship was created in the eleventh century, when the Celtic-Norse chieftain, Somerled, the progenitor of the MacDonalds, led a successful rising against the Viking ruler of the Western Isles. It was a time of warfare and pillage, and a period in which the Gaelic culture flourished. When pipers and poets were paid for their services and toured the castles and strongholds. The same traditions were carried forward to the crofting communities of later centuries, and survive even today in the work of the best Gaelic poets.

The Lordship lasted for nearly 400 years until 1493 when King James IV of Scotland took the Western Isles into his Edinburgh-based realm. The end of the fifteenth century also marked the beginning of the prolonged attack on Gaelic culture, which had spread as far as Aberdeenshire and to Edinburgh itself.

During much of this period, from 1373 to 1838, South Uist was effectively owned by the Clanranald family. The last Clanranald sold his ancestral lands in the nineteenth century to Col. John Gordon of Cluny. By this time, Clanranald was no longer the generous protector of his flock of clansmen. In common with Lochiel and the MacDonalds and MacLeods of Skye, he had made the awful transition from Gaelic aristocrat to capitalist landowner.

The following Gaelic song, 'In Praise of Uist', was sung at the time of the Clearances.

> *O my country, I think of thee, fragrant, fresh Uist of the handsome*
> *youths, where nobles might be seen, where Clan Ranald has*
> *his heritage.*
> *Land of bent grass, land of barley, land where everything is*
> *plentiful, where young men sing songs and drink ale.*
> *They come to us, deceitful and cunning, in order to entice us from*
> *our homes; they praise Manitoba to us, a cold country without*
> *coal or peat.*
> *I need not trouble to tell you it; when one arrives there one can see*
> *– a short summer, a peaceful autumn, and long winter of bad*
> *weather.*
> *If I had as much as two suits of clothes, a pair of shoes and my fare*
> *in my pocket, I would sail for Uist.*

It is fair to say that on South Uist, as on most other Highland estates, the relationship between the landowner and the community is still in the post-1745 stage in which the interests of the laird – or even the syndicate – take precedence. Surprisingly few islanders are prepared to say this is a bad thing.

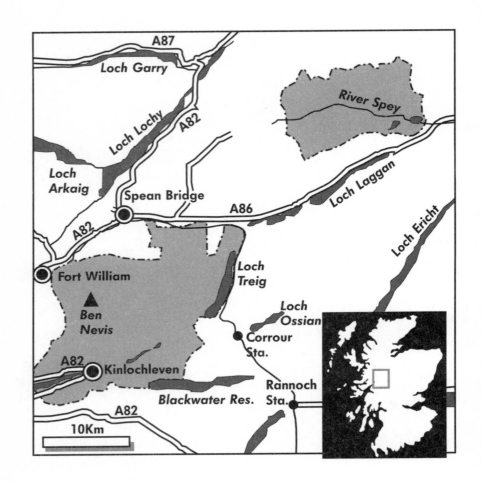

ACREAGE – 135,000
OWNER – BRITISH ALCAN
MANAGED FOR – HYDRO-ELECTRICITY, SPORT
POINTS OF INTEREST – INCLUDES PART OF BEN NEVIS, AONACH
MOR SKI CENTRE, MAMORE MOUNTAINS

CHAPTER EIGHT

Alcan Highland Estates

T he snow which is beginning to drive down the strath, swirling
in a bitterly cold wind, will melt into Spey Dam and be turned
back against the lie of the land to flow as water into the west.
Since the 1940s, when Canadian mining engineers tunnelled from
Loch Crunachdan down through the hills to Kinlochlaggan, and Loch
Laggan, a natural Highland watershed has been overcome by human
engineering.

A significant proportion of the headwaters of the Spey, which
should flow to the Moray Firth, is gathered at the start of a great
network of dams, pipes and shafts and carried 35 miles to Fort
William to provide the electricity to smelt aluminium. Along the way,
potential energy is harnessed from the Laggan Dam and Loch Treig
across the River Spean, from which a 4.5-metre tunnel was drilled for
15 miles through the shoulder of the Ben Nevis range. This enormous
undertaking, which began in 1924, involved 2,000 workers and the
laying of 20 miles of railway.

The single reason for the great effort? To secure for an aluminium
company its own electricity supply. For the past 60 years, British
Alcan – the name has changed along the way – has been one of the
biggest landowners in Scotland. It holds 135,000 acres in two large
sections, and gathers water from a much larger surrounding area.

It is almost certain that such a scheme would not be accepted today, but hydro-engineering was carried out on a grand scale in Scotland at the time, and the First World War had exposed a great need for the versatile, light metal.

Up where it all begins, the water does have an odd look to it. It may be that the wind is coming down the strath over the old drove road of the Corrieyairick and rippling the water surface in a west and northwards direction, or it may just be my imagination, but when I look at the water of Spey Dam I feel as if it wants to flow in another direction. It seems odd that some of it should be siphoned off to plunge westwards.

The great waterworks have buried many old constructions and made strange others. Just before Glenshirra shooting-lodge, there is a small Wade's bridge set at an odd angle to the raised road from Laggan. It is a remnant of the days before the dam, now going nowhere in a grassy sward which is often flooded by water. Back at the mouth of the loch there are the remains of the village of Crathie, once home to 200 people. Three of the last strath dwellers are still alive, living elsewhere in the Highlands.

But this is now a largely empty place, albeit that it is home to four of the six estate employees on Alcan's 135,000 acres. An unimpressive employment figure, you might think, for the acreage of land involved. On the neighbouring state-owned Creag Meagaidh National Nature Reserve – run by Scottish Natural Heritage – there are three full-time employees on 10,000 acres.

Alcan employs three stalkers, two maintenance staff and a head shepherd. The figure does not, of course, include the farming and crofting tenants on the estates of Killiechonate and Mamore – which you might be surprised to learn include part of Ben Nevis, Britain's highest mountain.

The east-most section, which contains the Spey Dam, is called Glenshirra and Sherramore, and operates as a sporting and electricity strath, looked after by estate factor Richard Sidgwick, a well-whiskered, well-spoken, tweed-clad gent whose father worked for the company and was factor in the same place in the 1960s. He is obviously proud of the place, confident it is being run to the best of

A lone rowan in the unnaturally treeless landscape of Assynt estate
(Glyn Satterley)

The remote Carnmore lodge in the heart of the Letterewe estate
(Glyn Satterley)

Bleached branches, stripped bare by deer, in a struggling Mar Lodge forest
(Glyn Satterley)

The heart of the problem: a red deer stag among two-hundred-year-old pine trees on Mar Lodge. No saplings have survived since the eighteenth century (Scottish National Heritage)

The Duke of Buccleuch on Bowhill estate
(Glyn Satterley)

Cameron of Lochiel: the archetypal
Highland laird poses by the River
Arkaig (Glyn Satterley)

The Duke of Atholl on a pheasant-shoot in front of Blair Castle (Glyn Satterley)

Letterewe lodge on Loch Maree, the gateway to Paul van Vlissinger's 87,000 acres (Glyn Satterley)

Dunrobin Castle, a useful asset for Sutherland (Glyn Satterley)

Deer-stalking on Ben Armine, part of the
Sutherland estates (Glyn Satterley)

A pearl-fisher on the River Spey. The salmon
river is a major source of income for Seafield
estate (Glyn Satterley)

LEFT:
Environment-friendly crofting on the shell-rich
soils of South Uist (Glyn Satterley)

ABOVE:
Glen Nevis on Alcan estate: used as a location for the film *Braveheart*, despite a landscape much altered since the thirteenth century (Glyn Satterley)

LEFT:
The barren upper reaches of Glenfeshie estate: a dying pine forest, hillside erosion and a bulldozed road for stalking — all on the Cairngorm National Nature Reserve (Scottish National Heritage)

his abilities, and in the best traditions (a common phrase among factors) of Highland estate management.

When I met Sidgwick for the first time, in his offices in Fort William's High Street, he remarked that the word 'factor' was no longer appropriate, associated as it was with sinister intent. He prefers to think of himself as a chartered surveyor and the managing agent. Whatever. The staff and the tenants will continue to think of him as the factor. His aim, in managing the non-electricity side of the property, is simply to 'make ends meet', and he admits that in the past year he has just about achieved his aim.

Balancing the books should be made slightly easier on this estate – and on most estates with an urban fringe – by the developments around Fort William. After all, the 'let portfolio', which he says is the backbone of any Highland estate, includes a whisky distillery and the Aonach Mor ski resort. Lochaber District Council leases the ski mountain, and sub-leases it to the operator. Then there is a regular income from the use of the estates as a military training ground.

Sidgwick stresses, however, that the sole reason for owning the land is to have a secure, and cheap, electricity supply. The power wrought from the land comes first and its protection has resulted, for example, in detailed agreements between the ski centre and the company over the maintenance of two of the 11 water inlet shafts between Loch Treig and Fort William.

On a cold January day, I met Sidgwick to look at the sporting end of the operation, the part of the estate which the factor suggested would be easiest for me to inspect. We met at Glenshirra lodge, as the snow began to lie and thoughts turned to the value of four-wheel drive vehicles and the likely state of the A9 for the journey home.

The lodge was well chilled, it had not been occupied for several months, but it was crisp, clean and recently decorated. It is redecorated every three or four years at a cost of around £8,000 – if the aluminium profits can stand it.

It is much more luxurious, for example, than Atholl's Forest Lodge in Glen Tilt, and seemed to me to be too big for the ten visitors which Sidgwick said it would sleep 'comfortably'. 'It caters for a nice size of party,' he said with a confident smack.

Built in Victorian times as a shooting lodge for the Ramsden family, which once owned a huge acreage (descendants retain the 42,000-acre Ardverikie estate on south Loch Laggan), its use is now confined to the months of May to October, when English and Belgian shooting parties visit. Alcan itself uses the property for management meetings in the watery wilderness.

Oddly, the stalking was not let on this section of the estate until 1983. The stalkers themselves did all the shooting and, local rumour has it, made a good living on the side through the sale of stalking and meat.

Now, it is a deer forest with an unusual ratio – in wider Scottish terms – of stags to hinds. There are around 140 stags to 100 hinds, which compares very favourably with other deer forests on which hinds can vastly outnumber stags.

Sidgwick is confident the numbers are right, and the stags in Glenshirra are probably not complaining, given the unusual level of protection they enjoy. There are 14 blocks of plantation forestry, covering 2,000 acres, and scattered in apparently random and certainly unnatural fashion along the strath. The fences are breached, deliberately, in all of them. The blocks were designed, Sidgwick claimed, as part of an integrated forestry and sporting strategy.

'I don't mind sacrificial areas as long as the whole thing is in balance,' he observed, as we stopped in the gathering snow to watch some very healthy-looking stags on the edge of a patch of Scots pine and European larch. The animals were on the open ground just outside the forest – the fence behind them was missing – and they were on the lee side of the woodland.

The deer are fed a mix of concentrates and whole sugar-beets in the winter, primarily to stop them from wandering down the glen and into farmland where they are likely to be shot. The strategy seems to be working. Farmer Donnie Wilson, who lives just outside the estate boundary, one of the last farmers in the upper strath, remarked to me earlier the same day, almost with a tinge of regret, that there had been no deer marauding in his fields of late.

Despite the factor's assurance, the whole thing did not look as if it was in balance. At the very least, it could not be called a natural system, or even an ideal artificial system. The plantations are relatively dense, offering limited open space for the animals, and the deer have stripped the bark from many of the lower branches and browsed up to the height they can reach on their hind legs. As a result, the plantation edges looked ragged and scruffy, even if it was good to see deer with shelter. The woodland will provide shelter, as long as it is not felled, but has no commercial value as timber in its present usage. Felling it would damage the deer. Sidgwick commented that there was no over-population of deer on most of the west coast estates, that the same number of deer had been shot each year for many years. The figure at Glenshirra and Sherramore was around 90 stags on each beat, 125 hinds and 20 to 30 calves.

Such justification of present shooting numbers is common currency, despite the obvious fact that in biological terms there must be over-population if there is no forest regeneration. There may not be an over-population in sporting terms. After all, deer are the mainstay after the water is gathered.

Through the sporting lets the company attempts to make enough money in just seven weeks' stag-stalking to justify paying the wages of three stalkers year-round, and to make a surplus, if possible. What is the attraction of this landscape for the Belgian party which visits every year?

'People come for the numbers of deer and the open stalking. Here they see hundreds of deer. A party of four might shoot 15 to 20 stags in a week.'

By contrast, a week's stalking in the natural woods of the Czech Republic might produce no more than one or two stags per shooter, per week. And yet the sport in eastern Europe can cost twice as much as it does in Scotland. The reason for the price difference? I would like to think it is because of the high standard of the habitat, the appreciation of wild woodlands and wild creatures (the deer are much heavier), and the thrill of a hunt which must feel more like a real wilderness experience than the essentially bare stalking of the Scottish hills.

As we drove further up the road, the factor's Audi estate beginning to slip a little, I could not help imagining a verdant pine and birch forest in far Bohemia; a home (still) to eagles, wolves and wild boar, as well as the red deer. In front of me, the strath was just bleakness.

Further up the glen was a reminder of days gone by and a time when the Corrieyairick Pass was a major drove route for men taking their stock to the south and the great trysting place of Falkirk. The road through the pass, still passable by four-wheel drive, was built by General Wade, and he had a barracks created for his men at Garvamore.

The building, a monument of considerable interest to Historic Scotland, was in relatively sound condition, but for the roof. It was covered with a red tarpaulin held down by ropes. The tarpaulin kept the water out while the barracks awaited an uncertain future. Alcan was interested in opening the site as a tourist attraction in 1988, but the estimated cost of renovation was around £270,000. The multi-national company was prepared to pay £60,000, and hoped the rest would come from grants from the regional council and Historic Scotland. In the event, the idea was defeated by one vote on the council and the windows have since been boarded up. 'My instructions are to maintain it,' said Sidgwick.

While the barracks might survive a few years more, their surroundings have not been enhanced by electricity ownership. Next to the red-topped monument were two ugly metal sheds which were erected to feed and shelter the 1,300 sheep on the estate. A small area of pine had recently been planted by the edge of the road – a popular walking route in summer – in the hope that it would eventually screen the buildings from passers-by.

On the subject of livestock, Sidgwick expressed himself very pleased with the 106 per cent lambing rate, which he attributed to the skill of his shepherd. The figure was helped along by the fact that, unusually, all the sheep are inside extensive stock fences on the side of the hill, making their collection and protection much easier.

After the stalking, forestry is the main business and there is a small aluminium-roofed sawmill in the strath. ('We have a penchant for aluminium roofs, although I prefer corrugated iron. If a branch falls on the aluminium, it will go straight through it.') The mill made a surplus of around £30,000 in 1994 through the local sale of timber for fencing and building, and provides the estate's needs. Most of the production was based on larch from a mature plantation on the north side of the strath. The factor said a ford would be created on the upper Spey to allow another patch to be removed.

Like most traditionally schooled estate factors, Sidgwick prefers exotic trees, on the not-surprising basis that there is a market for the product. He believes the Forestry Commission's woodland grant scheme payments for the regeneration and planting of pine and birch woods will 'certainly improve the diversity of wildlife', but will not produce timber of value. Scots pine, he claimed, can take 130 years to produce decent saw logs. Timber production is one of his hobby-horses.

'The Forestry Commission was told to replenish the fellings of both world wars and to create a large-scale forest. Under Labour in the 1970s, the tax was 98p. So if you spent £1 it cost you 2p. It did help create a national asset. The country was planting 33,000 hectares annually. It then dropped with the change in the tax system in 1988 to 9–10,000 ha. Our imports cost £12 billion a year. There is no doubt the old regime served the nation, and private individuals, very well.

'But we have now had seven years in which far less timber has been planted. In 45 years time there will be a real shortfall. Politicians don't give a damn about 45 years time. Short-term issues are all that matter. At best, they think about the next election.'

Despite his misgivings about the native woodland schemes – and he is right, there is no useful market at present – the estate is heavily involved in grant-aided regeneration projects. On the south side of the strath, on the hillside which marches with the neighbouring 'green' estate of Creag Meagaidh, there is a Site of Special Scientific Interest – for montane plants – which has become the subject of a large birch woodland scheme, albeit dependent on deer-fencing.

An even bigger scheme was in the pipelines for Caol, on both sides of Loch Leven. Stretching to nearly 2,000 acres, and running around the head of the loch, the intention was to create regenerating woodland without the use of fencing. The factor was not over-optimistic about its benefits. 'It would give much better deer wintering,' he said, 'but they won't be allowed to winter because they will be shot by the people of Kinlochleven.'

Poaching by the good folk of Kinlochleven – a place built for aluminium and no other particularly good reason, with a community with a high unemployment rate – was a sore subject. The natives have no claim to the native wildlife.

As we drove back down the strath, defeated by the snow while we were still several miles from the Corrieyairick, I asked about two empty cottages sitting by the river. They were once occupied by staff, but would now cost a considerable amount to repair. Sidgwick said he was not a great lover of holiday cottages, which he saw as a big management burden, particularly if there was no estate wife happy to do the cleaning and laundry between each visit. And, while a holiday cottage might take £3,000 a year, after administration costs, someone could live in the place – an estate employee or someone connected with the estate – pay a guaranteed £2,000 a year and be there all the time.

Generally, the estate prefers to choose estate staff with families, but the policy is made difficult by the continuing depopulation of the area and the distance to school and friends. At the time of my visit, one stalker was leaving for exactly that reason.

We ended the visit at Sherramore Lodge, across from Glenshirra Lodge, another Victorian shooting property now used by estate staff. Sidgwick showed me the spick and span larder – meeting EU standards – where the deer are cut and cleaned after the stalk, pointed out the health and safety manual, and remarked that Alcan brought to estate ownership the safety standards of the advanced industrial world. Stalkers had even been given winter survival courses. The houses were in good repair.

Back in the west, across the watershed and around the town of Fort William, one of those Highland places with a lucrative tourist industry despite its own best efforts to offer a surprisingly large choice of poor service, bad food and little entertainment, Alcan

Highland Estates are reasonably well regarded. There are two golf courses on their land for which the take the grand annual rent of £25 each, and they have a fairly positive access policy over Ben Nevis, Glen Nevis and most of their land, although they were criticised in 1994 for wanting to prescribe marked paths for walkers during the crucial stag-stalking season. The local Scottish Natural Heritage office is broadly complimentary about the estate management in terms of its effect on conservation and access.

Naturally, each year thousands of visitors trample on the great mountain ranges, particularly Ben Nevis, the summit of which was sold to the John Muir Trust in March 2000. Before the sale, all the land above 2,000ft was leased by Alcan from the Fairfax-Lucy family, the owners of the mountain since the 1830s. Now Britain's highest mountain can be managed with conservation, not aluminium, in mind. There is room for improvement.

In 1994, SNH carried out a study of the Ben Nevis Site of Special Scientific Interest, which covers an area of 100 square kilometres and is regarded as nationally important for its geology and its nature conservation interests. Within this apparently precious area, the key land uses are forestry, agriculture, deerstalking and leisure and recreation.

The area is home to the red fox, pine marten, mountain hares, numerous birds of prey, and – according to a 24-hour count during the survey – 467 red deer. The conclusion was that SNH should continue to monitor Ben Nevis and should consider specific studies on the success, or otherwise, of breeding birds and the effects of the present grazing levels. Woodland, said the authors, was restricted mainly to Glen Nevis and some craggy slopes along the northern boundary of the site – the few places out of reach of grazing deer.

This report was hardly outwardly critical, but it contains clues to what is happening throughout the Highlands, and has been for centuries: a slow process of declining biodiversity, including the replacement of dwarf-shrub communities with coarse grass swards and the ongoing loss of surviving native woodland.

Not yet the ideal for a national park.

Elsewhere, the estate is user-friendly when it comes to the release of land for housing. There are as many as six property sales a year, usually house sites, and the key concern is only to avoid any impact on electricity generation. 'It is pretty soul-destroying for local people if they can't buy land locally for housing. If we had a policy of no disposals, it would stifle people's development and their ambitions to own their own homes,' said Sidgwick.

By contrast – an argument against state ownership? – there is no doubt it would normally be harder to win a bit of land from the Forestry Commission. There are many tales from the same area of the west coast of people seeking to buy a small woodland next to a community for local benefit, or a piece of ground for a house, only to come up against the sitka plantation-like impenetrability of FC bureaucracy.

Even the 'sinister' factor, one step removed from the real landowner, is more accessible than the civil servant.

Sidgwick offers no illusions on the subject of agriculture in the Highlands, nor on the future direction of land-ownership. 'Agricultural enterprises in the Highlands don't generate substantial money for reinvestment. I can't think of a single estate where sufficient income is made to reinvest in repairs which are not running repairs.'

Selling bits of the family silver, the odd deer forest here, the lochside acre there, is the only way for large sporting estates, like Alcan and Lochiel, to survive, according to the man who factors both properties. 'Anybody who thinks that owning a Highland estate is an easy way of preserving their inheritance is wrong.'

What about the place of the factor? 'You are not going to get owners of estates in the Highlands to deal with the day-to-day running of the estates. Where estates are run by absentee lairds, they are usually away because they have to work nowadays, they work in Edinburgh or in London to generate money to fund the estate. And somebody who has to earn a living as a banker in London will not be able to devote the attention that a competent agent on the ground can.

'Inevitably, the next generation have to be absentee owners because very few can make their living in the area, although I can think of a number of next generation landowners who do manage to operate within 20 miles of Inverness. There are very few people who have the inclination to live in the west Highlands seven days a week, 52 weeks in the year.'

Could he, sadly, be right about this: that because there are few individuals who want to live in the place or can make a living in the place, there is little alternative to the increasingly absent owner, possibly the Danish forestry investor, or the old declining clan estate? Or is it the case that the current lack of enterprise and people in Highland glens is a function of the failure of the estate system itself, and of national and local government and their agencies to provide the right investment and the right incentives? Perhaps the truth is in a mingling of the two. For example, Sidgwick admits he sees over-grazing 'everywhere', but like many other critics of the hill livestock payments, believes there is no alternative. He sees sheep subsidies as a form of social payment.

Surely there must be other, more productive, ways of restoring social and environmental vitality to the Highland glens.

In the meantime, it is nothing more than the creation of aluminium which forms the bedrock policy of this huge area of land. It explains why the estate buys only Land Rovers – one of the company's biggest customers – and why the factor has to use aluminium roofing on his outbuildings. And it explains why there is more money one year than there is the next to invest in non-running repairs. Inevitably, the international metals market has a knock-on effect on the management.

It also explains why the company resisted many requests to co-operate with the ski development on Aonach Mor, until a point, according to sources at the Nevis Range company, at which public pressure and the declining job prospects in Fort William pushed them into the successful venture.

The town had become an unemployment blackspot, losing 2,000 jobs with the closure of its pulp mill, and 1,400 jobs as Alcan trimmed its workforce over the years to the present level of around 300. The good, but short, summer tourist trade was never going to be enough to support a decent local economy, and winter sports were seen as a potential boost to the wealth of the town.

In fact, they have been just that, although the ski company continues to find the factory difficult to deal with and, in the summer of 1995, was less than convinced that the £250,000 gravel filter which it was obliged to install to safeguard water intakes was necessary. The filter was part of the original deal which sought, in great detail, to prevent any damage to the precious water asset.

The story of aluminium in the Highlands began in the last century, when the new business of producing the light metal using electrolysis required huge amounts of power. The prodigious rainfall of the west, and its mountain topography, made perfect partners for the enterprise.

The British Aluminium Co Ltd was created in 1894 and two years later the first smelter was opened at Foyers on the eastern shore of Loch Ness. The plant was capable of satisfying one tenth of the world demand for aluminium, which at the time was 2,000 imperial tons a year.

The company opened another two smelters, at Kinlochleven in 1907, and at Lochaber outside Fort William in 1929. By the 1930s, aluminium was used worldwide in a wide range of engineering and household goods, and by 1943 the waters of upper Speyside had been diverted and the system still in place today was complete.

Every year, a total of 200 billion gallons of water pours through the turbines which create electricity for the Lochaber plant. It comes from four dams, a series of tunnels and aqueducts, and some from the eastern watershed, and it ends its long journey when it is discharged to the River Lochy and the Atlantic.

The Kinlochleven plant, built between 1904 and 1909, remains the smallest and oldest (Foyers closed in the 1960s) smelter in the world, specialising in high purity aluminium. Its electricity is supplied thanks to the eight-mile-long Blackwater Reservoir on the west side of Rannoch Moor.

During a modernisation programme in 1981, when there was a

worldwide cutback in smelting capacity due to market conditions, around £40 million was invested in Lochaber. The Fort William operation is not in immediate danger, but Kinlochleven will have closed by the turn of the millennium. After they have gone, both schemes will leave behind power stations, employing a few people and producing electricity.

In Highland terms, nearly 100 years of continuous operation will not have been a bad innings.

Even if, in the same century, the land which made the profits possible has seen an increase in deer numbers, the spread of discredited one-species forestry, the decline of the few surviving remnants of native woodland, and increased damage to the hills caused by the growing demand for recreation. In common with much of the Highlands.

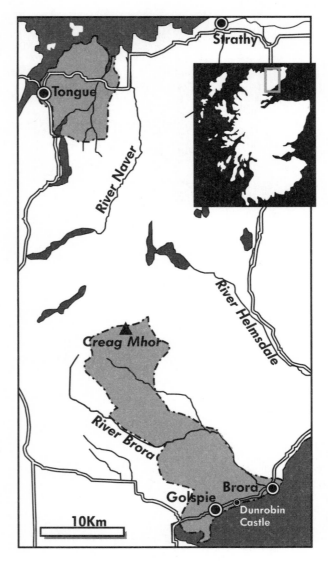

ACREAGE – 90,000
OWNER – COUNTESS OF SUTHERLAND, LORD STRATHNAVER
MANAGED FOR – TOURISM, SPORT, FORESTRY
POINTS OF INTEREST – FAMILY DESCENDED FROM NOTORIOUS
CLEARING DUKE

CHAPTER NINE

Sutherland Estate

I found it after 40 minutes walking in ever-widening circles. Just when I was about to curse the directions I had been given in the pub in Golspie the night before, I struck another forest road. This time it felt right.

Within five minutes it led through the pines to a great, square monument. The pillars supporting the classical roof were faced with granite, and six steps led to a red and grey granite diamond-patterned floor in front of a tablet inscribed to the memory of James Loch.

The words are easily read, 135 years after they were carved: 'To the honourable memory of James Loch, who loved in the serene evening of his life to look around him here.

'May his children's children gather here and think of him, whose life was spent in virtuous labour for the land he loved, for the friends he served, who have raised these stones.'

Looking around today reveals nothing but the interior of the pine plantation, which must be around 40 years old, and encircles the monument. Faint, grassy forest paths meet at the statue, but look as if they carry little traffic. There is no sign that people visit the monument today. Perhaps that is the idea.

In the nineteenth century, it would have stood prominently on this hill above the A9; Dunrobin Castle would have been clearly visible, as would a better-known statue, that of the first Duke of Sutherland, whose memory is still deprecated in this Clearance county, and whose huge stony likeness stands on Beinn a'Bragaidh above Golspie. The figure is known locally as 'the mannie'.

James Loch was Commissioner to the house of Sutherland, a Lowlander, lawyer and local MP who was instrumental in the infamous Sutherland Clearances of 1812–19. With the factor Patrick Sellar, he was the instrument of the first Duke of Sutherland's drive to improve his land by removing 5,000 folk from the populous glens and replacing them with sheep farmers from the Borders and flocks of black-faced ewe and north-country Cheviot. The sheep are there yet today.

The day before my discovery in the wood, I had visited the Strathnaver Museum in old Farr Church at Bettyhill. The museum has a useful display on the Clearances, written and drawn in brilliant colours by pupils of the local primary and secondary schools, who are not being allowed to forget.

One of the posters quotes Loch himself, who had a track record of improving land in Moray. The children recall the words penned by Loch to describe their own ancestors: '. . . such a set of savages is not to be found in the wilds of America. If Lord and Lady Stafford [as the duke was then called] do not put it in my power to quell this banditti, we may bid adieu to all improvement.' Such comments notwithstanding, the monument remembers his labour as virtuous.

In John Prebble's *The Highland Clearances*, the same Loch is described as a man 'hated as few men have been hated'; a man who was convinced of the need to pull the people of Sutherland out of the past by the scruff of their necks. He found them slothful and dirty, living side by side with their animals – to the mutual warmth of both – and blamed the potato for making their existence too easy. The humble tattie 'enabled them with less labour than before to raise what was sufficient for the maintenance of their families, their pigs and their poultry'.

Clearly, this was a backward population in need of improvement; in place of the natives, there would be 40 sheep farmers.

It was pleasing to find the Loch memorial, to be pointed to a little-known detail from the Clearances, like a speck of gold found in the sparse Strath of Kildonan. Little enough is known about the real detail of the Clearances, and what is known has been swirled around and examined, and forgotten, under a thousand lights.

I had enjoyed another diverting nugget at Farr Church. The minister at the time that Strathnaver was cleared was the Revd David Mackenzie, who was appointed by the estate and served all his 54 years as the Church of Scotland minister at Farr, where he was ordained in 1813.

He preached the gospel according to the Sutherland family – the estate decided on the form of worship, and chose the minister – and he told the God-fearing families brutally evicted from their homes that they were being rightly punished for their sins. He translated the English of Loch and other agents into Gaelic, and told the tenants it was God's will that they go. On one occasion, his Farr Church held as many as 2,000 people whose houses had been destroyed in the glens. They were sheltering before moving on to the Americas, to the slums of the big cities to the south, or to the bare rocky coast nearby which the estate had kindly made available, in the hope of forcing the people to become crofter/fishermen. The lack of proper harbours and the lack of experience of the people on the sea meant that in the first ten years of settlement, more than 100 boats were wrecked along the coast.

In that church, in the hours when the old, sick and the young were presumably confused and wretched, the Revd Mackenzie told them they should leave without complaint. Like Loch, he saw them as a dirty, whisky-making rabble, even if they were God-fearing.

The 'nugget' was simply the fact that the fine, grey, granite plinth, which stood atop the Revd Mackenzie's gravestone outside the church, fell off its pedestal some years ago. The museum curator told me this as if it had just happened.

In fact, it has lain so long, exactly where it fell, that the ground is claiming it and the grass is now beginning to creep over the last exposed surface. No one wanted to pick up the plinth and have it restored. Like Loch's monument in the middle of the plantation, it is no longer tended; another embarrassing reminder.

But it is not just those who live in Sutherland who are ready to recall the Clearances. Lord Stafford has his admirers, even today.

I arrived at Bettyhill – possibly named after Elizabeth, first Countess of Sutherland – soon after *The Daily Telegraph* columnist, Auberon Waugh, had chosen to revisit the subject. He wrote that the Duke, Sellar and Loch had done us all a favour, and we should appreciate them today for that. The blasphemous column caused a row in Sutherland, and a copy of the article was pinned to a door in the museum. No additional comment was necessary.

In the bar of the Sutherland Arms Hotel in Golspie there is a regular having a pint. He asks me – as he no doubt asks every lone traveller in the place – what I am doing and where I am going. The mention of a book on land-owning, and a meeting with Lord Strathnaver the following morning, invokes an immediate reference to the trial of Patrick Sellar and the fact that he escaped punishment in Inverness. Sellar was found Not Guilty of culpable homicide, real injury and oppression.

The trial might have happened in the past few weeks, for all the vehemence of the man at the bar. This is a peculiar phenomenon in Sutherland, which does not spread to the neighbouring county of Caithness, a place relatively free of Clearances. No one, for example, has suggested changing the name of Loch Street in Wick.

There is, however, a battle over that 100ft-high statue on top of Beinn a'Bragaidh. The former SNP councillor Sandy Lindsay, from Kingussie, has been fighting a battle to have the statue removed, backed by sympathisers in this country and from as far afield as Australia. If his efforts have done nothing else, they have stirred the embers of the Sutherland Clearances once again, bringing new heat to a fire which will not be allowed to die.

A large part of the enmity towards the statue is caused by the inscription, which outdoes the good press given to Loch on his monument. The Clearing Duke is described as '. . . a judicious, kind and liberal landlord, who identified the improvement of his vast estates with the prosperity of all who cultivated them'.

Furthermore, he would '. . . open his hands to the distress of the widow, the sick and the traveller'. And, the unkindest cut in the rock, the pillar was said to have been erected in 1834 by 'a mourning and grateful tenantry'. Sons and daughters, no doubt, of the thousands who watched their homes burned down as they were brutally evicted from Strathnaver and the other glens.

Today, the Sutherland family is fed up with the Clearances, and with being held responsible for its ancestors. This is hardly surprising, and yet it is hard to drive through the area without thinking of these events. It is possible that an 80-year-old today might have had a grandparent cleared from Strathnaver. It happened not so long ago – long enough to be history, and recent enough to be part of the common consciousness. But should the sins of the fathers be visited on their sons, and distant relatives?

As I left the museum at Farr, the caretaker remarked that I could not write about Sutherland without mentioning the Clearances.

I drove to Golspie by way of Strathnaver itself, the glen where one Donald Macleod, a stonemason, witnessed the clearance of Rosal, and was himself moved from the strath. The event made a great impression on him and he immortalised what he saw in his book, *Gloomy Memories*. The year before he died, in 1857, he wrote: 'I have devoted all my spare time and means, for the last 34 years, expostulating, remonstrating with, and exposing the desolators of my country, and extirpators of my race, from the land of their birth . . . considering that I could not serve God in a more acceptable way than to help those who could not help themselves.'

On my way through Strathnaver, the greenest furrow in the region, and once settled in 12 separate townships, I stopped to look at the memorial which stands by the side of the road, in memory of Macleod. It is across the River Naver from the site of Rosal. The old place is not visible from the road today: the view is of a forestry plantation, which comes almost to the edge of the river. There is snow on the ground, and the chaffinches and the trickling water are the only sounds. There is no hint of a ghost in this cold place.

The inscription on my third clearance monument could not be simpler. 'In memory of Donald Macleod, stonemason, who witnessed the destruction of Rosal in 1814 and wrote *Gloomy Memories*. Erected by public subscription.' No vainglorious claims, no eulogies.

Strathnaver today has a few crofts and farm houses, but it remains relatively unpopulated. The only signs of life on a chill March day are the occasional parties of salmon anglers on the riverbank. I pass two four-wheel drive jeeps and a Mercedes estate, and see more cars of similar prestige parked in the small laybys made for fishing parties in search of spring salmon. No doubt the villagers of Rosal once took a good haul themselves.

Although they lived in earth-floored blackhouses, in which the smoke from the fire was crudely deflected by a board towards a small hole in the roof, there survive some warm accounts of life in the strath. There would be four or five families in each village, and they would have goats, sheep, horses and cattle, with fish from the river, their own butter and cheese and chicken, and potatoes and kail and milk. And, of course, the home-distilled whisky which was sold to raise extra money to pay the increasing rents.

Further down the road, by the shores of Loch Naver, a large number of hinds are heading towards the road; it is early evening with the light soon to fade, and they are making for the loch shore and the better grazing and shelter among the birch trees.

They have been forced together into large groups by the dense forestry plantations on the hillside. Deer kept out of trees. Trees planned without thought for deer. Birch which are dying. A typical Highland scene.

Strathnaver no longer belongs to the Sutherland family.

Do the Clearances resonate today in Highland politics? Alastair Strathnaver, a tall and handsome man who looks like a policeman, and once was, tells me they do. Among politicians in the main.

The Labour MP Brian Wilson protested some years ago about the fact that the Countess of Sutherland was president of the Gaelic Mod. She stepped down. Should the descendants of those responsible for trying to wipe out the Gaelic culture (as some claim of the Clearances) be allowed to officiate over its annual jamboree? Lord Strathnaver offered the organisers of the 1995 Mod in Golspie the use of Dunrobin

Castle for one or two concerts. The offer was not taken up.

Strathnaver admits he is tired of the whole affair. 'I think it is extraordinary that modern actions should be in any way affected by something which happened in a way which is still unclear to serious historians, 175 years, 170 years ago. I can't think of any other example of that in Britain. It is a discussion that is completely unsupportable.' He is right. The atrocities of Nazi Germany, much more recently, are not visited on decent Germans today.

He has had numerous experiences of the past being pushed into the present. For eight years the family seat at Dunrobin Castle, north of Golspie, was the subject of a hugely ambitious plan to create a luxury hotel, surrounded by a model, circa 1800, village, with tourist accommodation for 600. The deal involved a Swiss holiday company, the Highlands and Islands Development Board, Highland Regional Council and the Scottish Office. It fell apart when the Swiss company decided there was not enough in the way of matched funding from the UK agencies. It was said more than once at the time that the project should not be supported because of the family history.

'That was ludicrous. The whole point was to create economic opportunities for the people of east Sutherland. To knock that on the head for reasons of historical debate was nonsense.' He feels just as strongly – although he has not said so before in public – about the statue of the first duke on Beinn a'Bragaidh. 'It is a local landmark which people want to keep. A referendum would be 90 per cent in favour, 10 per cent against. Everybody in Golspie is livid that their favourite local landmark should be affected.' In any case, the land belongs to the estate, the approach road belongs to the estate. The campaign is a bit of popular mischief-making – seen from Dunrobin.

Strathnaver was born in London 'in the middle of the 1947 blizzards'. His parents thought it was safer, with the country paralysed by the weather, for his birth to take place in the civilised south. He was brought up near Dunrobin and attended school in Golspie before leaving to complete his education at school and university in England. He worked for ten years after university before returning to play a key role in the estate.

Oddly – for a Scottish laird, at any rate – he chose the police force. It was, he says, something he always wanted to do and he found it fascinating. He spent two and a half years as a bobby on the streets, and the same time again as a temporary detective constable. He then briefly tried chartered accountancy, on safer ground for the landed, before joining the computer company IBM for five years. He came back to Scotland when 'my parents thought it would be a good idea'.

He is a rarity in the Highlands. He is an owner who lives and works on the estate, and he says the operation 'just about washes its face'. 'Those of us who are resident would much rather see resident landowners who are permanently part of the community. But I also recognise that in many cases a loss-making sporting estate has got to be supported by economic activity elsewhere.

'Nobody has come up with a viable alternative which is not going to cost the taxpayer millions of pounds a year in state support. At the moment, I don't see a viable alternative.'

Strathnaver is highly active in Highland affairs, the Clearances notwithstanding. He was a commissioner with the Deer Commission, which is responsible for policy on all deer populations, and was formerly a regional board member of Scottish Natural Heritage – one of several lairds connected with SNH who are routinely criticised by radical environmentalists.

His views are not, however, those of the reactionary landowner. He has a great enthusiasm for change and for development, and is not in the least blinkered about the state of the land. He surprises me, after a drive inland from Dunrobin through Sutherland territory, by remarking that much of the land we saw was 'knackered'.

On the road to remote Ben Armine lodge he pointed out a large private lodgepole pine plantation which is quite white and half-dead, thanks to the pine beauty moth. The moorland road itself is surrounded for part of the way by a new plantation – planted by a private company on land sold by a crofter, who had exercised his right to buy his own property and sell for profit five years later. The crofter, who was lucky in having an unusually large croft – including hill land which would normally have been common grazing shared by several tenants – has all but retired on the proceeds.

The predecessor body to Scottish Natural Heritage objected to the scheme at the time because of growing concern over the afforestation of the peat country of the far north. The objection was overruled by the Scottish Office. It will eventually create an avenue of one form of mono-culture, providing access to another – the sporting interests of Ben Armine.

In this changing scene, looking away north towards the rolling peat country and the Skinsdale peatland Site of Special Scientific Interest – a large part of which is on his land – Strathnaver sees his principal role as a guarantor of continuity. Large estates can, it is true, practise good environmental and social management policies, not always following that most commercial avenue. They can, but they rarely do.

Ben Armine is a sporting estate with a remote lodge and a reputation as an excellent place for shooting and fishing. Its attractions, seeming like a land-locked island because of the peculiar discomfort of reaching it along a rough, eight-mile road, are understandable.

It boasts little, however, in the way of surviving native woodland, and the lodge itself is backed by a great fan of lodgepole pine, planted with no hope of commercial timber but as a shelter for deer. The estate's 25,000 hill acres provide employment for one gamekeeper. I know people with a dream of a different Highland landscape who would see long-term alternatives for such land, with fewer deer and more trees. But this northern landscape is not the Cairngorms and perhaps there is a sound argument in favour of continuing sporting management, based, at the very least, on fewer deer than are present today. Scottish Natural Heritage are concerned that throughout the north the encroaching forestry is pushing deer on to the Flow Country and the vast blanket bogs, where the damage is not caused by over-grazing, but by trampling of rare flora.

Such concerns are real to Strathnaver. The value of a landowner like him is that he sees the Highland landscape today, much of it, at any rate, is knackered, and something has to change.

He is not interested in laying the blame at the door of the landowner, however, claiming that we have come relatively recently to a proper understanding of the fact that extractive, mono-cultural forestry or sporting regimes, with too many deer and sheep, have left a legacy of environmental damage. Some would dispute this late recognition, arriving as if with *fin de siècle* enlightenment, and point out that much the same problems were being identified by Frank Fraser Darling and others many decades ago.

'I want to see the land properly worked and properly looked after and pulled back from the brink,' says Strathnaver. 'I am not bothered about the pattern of land-ownership, that is not important. It has been exploited by excess sheep numbers in the nineteenth century, it has been exploited since by excessive sheep and deer numbers and all sorts of extractive policies from The Forestry Commission.'

The root cause of the deer 'problem', he identifies as decades of misconception that 'the more hinds the merrier'. He reckons the media continue to exaggerate the scale of red deer over-population, and hopes that the work under way to scientifically assess the ideal relationship between deer and its habitat will somehow find a satisfactory solution to the numbers game.

On some estates, he suggests, the population is just right, on others there may be as many as 3,000 animals more than is healthy. Several years ago, Strathnaver instituted a massive, one-season cull of 1,500 animals on his own land.

'What makes sense is to reduce the proportion as much as one can, while still staying viable as a sporting estate. The number of stags you shoot depends on the size of the lodge, the number of keepers, the number of weeks it is possible to do it. It is nothing to do with ecology. Most estates base their cull on a historically defined figure.

'It is up to SNH to find a way of calculating what a particular piece of ground can support, and then a suitable compromise has to be found – if one exists – between sporting and ecological requirements.' He would like to see deer numbers reduced to a level which would allow natural regeneration, but he does not know if that is possible everywhere.

Most refreshingly – and oddly, for a landowner – he believes, as many conservationists do, that the trusty voluntary principle in countryside management has been tried and has failed in Scotland. The Government, he says, should get much more involved with prescriptive policies on land use.

He is also a strong supporter of the Assynt crofters. 'They have done a most amazing job, and I fully understand and sympathise with them. I am sure they will go from strength to strength.'

His own plans include the creation of a landscaped, Scots pine-dominated plantation in Dunrobin Glen, the replacement of the sitka plantation to the north of Dunrobin with mixed hardwoods, and the eventual restoration of the castle gardens which were laid out in 1850, and whose little box hedges planted that year are still thriving today.

He displays an almost boyish enthusiasm for Highland land-ownership, admitting he has a well-reined tendency towards 'pie-in-the-sky' ideas. He does not display the sort of arrogance which suggests he knows instinctively what is right. He is happy, privately, to criticise the head stalker of another estate for his wanton killing of birds of prey and his ludicrous promotion of huge deer numbers – all achieved while the absentee owner is abroad. And he admits there is such a thing as a bad landowner. Perhaps even in his own family history. He has discovered, more than once, that if being a Sutherland is not a reason for attacking him, then being a 'rich landowner' may be.

For example, he was criticised for allegedly accepting a large sum of money from his former part-time employers, SNH, in return for a management agreement over the sea loch, Loch Fleet, and the surrounding pine forest. The story as it first appeared suggested he was intent on cutting down a precious pinewood, and had to be stopped from this crime by the environment agency which he claims to support.

The real story was not so simple. He, along with SNH, wanted to see Loch Fleet turned into a National Nature Reserve in order to prevent its exploitation by cockle dredgers digging up the tidal flats and causing severe damage to shellfish and bird populations. SNH looked at the proposal and insisted that the neighbouring forest – not native, but a plantation dating back to the eighteenth century – should be included, on the basis of its interesting and rare woodland flora. A flower called one-flowered wintergreen occurs in the woodland at levels unheard of elsewhere. Strathnaver, meanwhile, had been planning to fell the site for timber, on the reasonable basis that it was a well-established plantation. In the circumstances, SNH was obliged to offer a management agreement and to compensate the estate for genuine profits lost.

Strathnaver insisted that the matter was dealt with by his factor, and took no part in the proceedings. But one individual with an axe to grind made sure the tale got to the press.

The Sutherland estates today are dramatically reduced from that period in the nineteenth century when the third duke was the biggest private landowner in Europe, with more than two million acres, including the whole of Sutherland's 1.8 million acres.

He reaped the rewards of the marriage of his grandparents Elizabeth, the Countess of Sutherland, to the Marquess of Stafford (the Clearing Duke), which linked the two great families north and south of the border. The Dunrobin guidebook records that in 1785, Elizabeth married an Englishman, 'a great English landowner and one of Europe's richest men'.

It adds, with restraint, that in the early nineteenth century, the Marquess and his wife 'proceeded to make large-scale improvements to Sutherland's communications, land and townships which involved the clearance of some 5,000 people from their ancestral dwellings. The Sutherland Clearances, together with other Highland Clearances, were bitterly resented and remain to this day the subject of many books and plays.'

When the guidebook later returns to the subject, it observes that the first duke used his great personal wealth, derived from the English Industrial Revolution, to 'virtually destroy the old ways of life in Sutherland by uprooting the pastoral inhabitants of the hills and glens and moving some of them to modern housing on the coast where they could earn better money working in industries which he himself had financed'.

It goes on: 'Much the same sort of thing is done today by town councils who uproot people from their old, shabby but neighbourly streets and place them in ultra-modern, clinically clean but often completely inhuman high-rise flats, usually against their will.' A simplistic modern interpretation which the family would do well to drop when it reprints the guidebook.

The Sutherlands – like the dukes of Atholl – can trace their ancestors back to Freskin de Moravia (a Flemish nobleman of the lands of Moray (Moravia)) in the twelfth century, and yet the hundreds of years of family history which pre-date the Clearances (the fifteenth and sixteenth earls, for example, were loyal to the English throne during the Jacobite rebellions) is forgotten in the modern reckoning.

The expansion of the estates finally stopped in 1828 when the Countess took over Reay Forest at Tongue from the bankrupt Mackay family.

Much of the family fortune, observes Strathnaver, was spent by the grandson of the Clearing Duke on capital works which today would be carried out by the state – roads, railways, harbours, bridges. Such benefits are forgotten by the populace, remarks the owner.

The third duke had the idea that his Scottish lands could be turned into a revitalised community based on industry, with sporting estates run for tourism. The result was huge land reclamation schemes in the Loch Shin and Forsinard areas. Vast areas of peat were converted into grassland and more than £500 million was spent in the process.

Did it work? 'Of course not,' says Strathnaver. 'The land is as it is today because it has been badly treated, and the way to reverse that is to get the wheel going back the other way.' The actions of duke three left duke four with no choice but to sell large areas of land. But he also contributed his own 'expertise' to furthering the decline of the family's fortune. He sold property in Scotland in order to buy land in Canada, reasoning that there was a much brighter future to be found across the Atlantic. In fact, the land he bought in Alberta proved unsuccessful for his agricultural projects and he sold it on. The purchaser struck Alberta's oil.

When the fifth duke died in 1963 he had no children and the Scottish titles passed to his niece, Elizabeth (Strathnaver's mother); the dukedom – a UK title – could not pass through a female line and went to John Egerton, fifth Earl of Ellesmere, a descendant of the second son of the first duke. He lives near St Boswells in the Borders.

The present countess, Strathnaver's mother, lives today with her husband, Charles Janson, at Tongue House.

Deprived of oil millions, the family today runs five distinct properties: Uppat Estate, including Uppat House, and two farms; Dunrobin Castle and policies; Dunrobin estate, with coastal farms, woodlands and hill ground; Dalreavoch Estate, an inland sporting estate with two large crofts, and Ben Armine. There is some property in Golspie, where holiday cottages have been converted to short tenancies which Strathnaver believes are a help to the chronic housing shortage in the area. Overall, the surviving Sutherland empire employs between 30 and 40 full- and part-time staff.

As you go inland, one estate marches with the other, forming a block of 80,000 acres from the North Sea shore at Dunrobin to the brown mass of the interior.

Lord Strathnaver, who won his title by the 20 minutes in which he preceded the birth of his twin, Martin, operates as local manager of the estate, with a particular interest in Dunrobin, where he lives near the castle with his second wife. His parents and several trustees head the operation, and Martin has returned from London to run Uppat Estate.

The properties are held in trust, which is hardly surprising given the great loss of lands and money over the last 150 years. 'People have trusts,' says Strathnaver, 'to stop young Lochinvar from doing something crazy.'

The jewel is the clifftop folly of Dunrobin Castle – whose white mass can be seen on a clear day from the Ptarmigan restaurant on Cairngorm – and which was built to mimic a French château. It was designed by the architect Sir Charles Berry, who had not long completed the Houses of Parliament, and he modelled it on a Loire château.

'It is totally out of place, that is what it was all about, it was ostentation,' says Strathnaver, recalling that the eighteenth-century castle was three-sided, and the château itself was created a century later. 'If you wanted to see a French château, you would go to the Loire, so people are mostly delighted that they come across this extraordinary edifice here.'

As you approach Golspie from the north, Dunrobin's odd turrets and minarets can be glimpsed over the top of a recently felled sitka plantation, which is scheduled to make way for more traditional hardwood planting. It was created, after the gale of 1953 blew down a 200-year-old beechwood, when the vogue was for great blocks of sitka to help the national demand for timber; it was a vogue which often made no sense in the areas available for planting.

170

The most northerly of Scotland's great houses, Dunrobin was built with local sandstone which seems white from a distance in the sunshine, and is bedded on hard granite. It has enjoyed continuous inhabitation, or parts of it have, since the early fifteenth century.

Today, with its odd museum of hunting trophies in the grounds, it attracts 60,000 visitors a year – a respectable total given its geography, making it the thirty-fifth most visited historic house in Britain, and the eighth most popular in Scotland – excluding National Trust for Scotland properties. It has achieved its present popularity since its opening to the public in 1972. For the previous seven years it was run as a boys' public school.

The museum, which began as a sort of Wendy House for the Earl of Sutherland's eldest son – it was a twenty-first birthday present – was extended in 1878 by the third duke to house his growing collection of natural history and geology.

It was the fifth duke and his duchess, however, who made the place the bizarre repository of twentieth-century bad taste which it is today. It is stuffed with hundreds of hunting trophies. There is a giraffe's head and neck standing on the floor to welcome the visitor, above which there is an elephant head; there are rhino tails, giant fish, crocodile, buffalo, zebra, Indian gaur, impala, reedbuck and many more, making it a remarkable record both of game-hunting fanaticism and the spread of the empire. And of astounding wealth. On one wall is a photograph of the SY *Catania*, which took the duke and duchess to Eritrea, Abyssinia and darkest India on their round-the-world safaris.

The museum was restored recently with £60,000, raised by the sale of a Celtic armlet in a transaction which is illustrative of how the balancing of the family finances has become more complicated on this ancient estate, as it has on every other old clan property in Scotland. (The gardens which were tended in 1850 by 35 gardeners, are today looked after by three.)

Some of the visitors to the museum find it in bad taste and register their complaints. But Strathnaver, who is not keen on shooting, succeeds in living comfortably with the museum. He does not accept guilt for the impala and the kudu, any more than he accepts guilt for the Clearances.

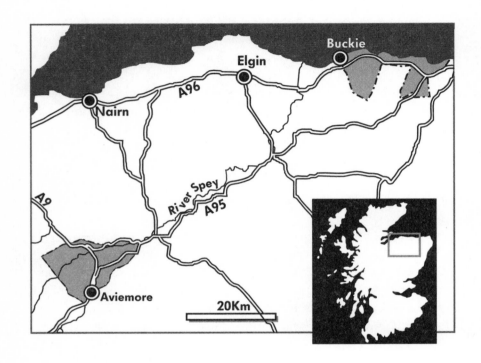

ACREAGE – 105,000
OWNER – EARL OF SEAFIELD, VISCOUNT REIDHAVEN
MANAGED FOR – SPORT, FORESTRY, FARMING
POINTS OF INTEREST – SON AND HEIR 'KIDNAPPED' BY FATHER
TO FREE HIM FROM A RELIGIOUS SECT

CHAPTER TEN

Seafield Estate

Seafield stretches from the corner of Aviemore through Grantown-on-Spey and north to Cullen and the Moray coast, and makes a particularly useful contribution to this study in that it was the only estate which refused to co-operate.

The factor, Brian Bedford, wrote to me on two occasions to politely decline my request for a meeting with Lord Seafield. The 59-year-old lord, who has no profession to his name, has an extremely low public profile, and there are a number of possible explanations for his apparent reluctance to talk. Tenants say that years can pass in Grantown, Boat of Garten and Carrbridge without anyone catching a glimpse of his lordship or his son, Viscount Reidhaven.

Indeed, the Seafield Estates are interesting for that very reason. If members of the public were stopped in a Glasgow or Edinburgh street and asked to name one of the big estates, or big landowners, it is highly unlikely anyone would mention Seafield. Atholl and Roxburgh might be contenders, as would Buccleuch and Balmoral, but there are precious few well-known estates in Scotland. Estates such as Atholl have been recipients over the years of much of the simplistic vilification by the press simply because they have not tried to duck the publicity.

Seafield is not the only estate which escapes national attention. The man on the street is not likely to mention Corrour, Balnagowan, Black Mount, Loyal, Strathconan, Ardverikie, Blackford or even the large Lochiel estates. There are hundreds of private estates in Scotland – including at least 500,000 acres owned by offshore companies or foreign businessmen – which have little or no public profile. This anonymity is particularly easy to maintain where the estate is largely unpopulated. Seafield, however, is well enough known in Speyside, and not well liked.

Having been denied the opportunity to see the property at first hand, the task of the journalist becomes somewhat easier. One resorts, in such instances, to the electronic cuttings libraries available in national newspaper offices, and to local comment. All but two of those approached on the subject of Seafield were highly critical.

One landowner, who knows both the laird and his factor, rolled his eyes towards the heavens and said: 'It is an appalling place. The factor is the founder member of the "never wrong" society, it is all that is worst about large private estates.

'I get the impression Lord Seafield is very resistant to the outside world. Removed from the real world. He has chosen a front man to do everything for him, the long-established device of large landowners. If you are an individual like that and have a fortune of £1 million to £10 million, most of which is not available but tied up in property, you buy in a sidekick and ask that individual to maximise the commercial opportunities. It is an entirely different ethic from that practised by the landowners on the Sutherland and Buccleuch estates.'

A local businessman in Aviemore was equally uncomplimentary: 'I have claimed on a number of occasions that the spirit of Patrick Sellar (the factor involved in the notorious Sutherland Clearances of last century) is alive and well and living on Speyside. The estate has been incredibly obstructive to our business.'

Several critics said the estate was run today as a business seeking to maximise income at every opportunity, with little obvious regard for the needs of the local community. Whether this is true is hard to say without hearing the voice of the estate's defence.

However, a quick glimpse at the cuttings points to other potential reasons for shyness. In 1992, the thirteenth Lord Seafield paid a team of former SAS men to rescue his son and heir, Viscount Reidhaven, from a religious sect. The young viscount, James Ogilvie-Grant, an old Etonian like his father, had been recruited to the Naqshbandi sect of Sufism in 1990, a mystical branch of the Muslim religion which was supported by the singer Cat Stevens.

According to one newspaper, Reidhaven adopted the name Sheik Abdul Qadir and fell under the influence of a charismatic 33-year-old Sufi named Muhammed Ali, whom he addressed as 'master'. He was said to have turned against his family.

There was a genuine fear on the estate, it was said, that the lands of Seafield and a family fortune might somehow pass to religious fanatics. Viscount Reidhaven was successfully removed from the sect and taken to the remote Knoydart peninsula on the west coast of Scotland where he spent three months receiving 'exit counselling' from American psychologists. One of the counsellors said the young aristocrat was 'not in a functional state of mind and had been manipulated in the extreme'. There are rumours on Speyside that, despite the best efforts of the American team, he later returned to the sect. His father has since remained silent on the subject.

To further complicate matters, one of the estates belongs to Reidhaven, and his absence therefore complicates its running, which is carried out by the local factor and by legal representatives in Edinburgh. Reidhaven is Lord Seafield's eldest son by his first marriage. In 1971 his lordship married his second wife, Egyptian Leila Refaat.

Another press cutting raises questions over the environmental ethics of the estate. At an industrial tribunal in 1994, the former head keeper, George Dey, claimed unfair dismissal after being sacked for slashing the tyres of a poacher's van and taking gulls' eggs. Taking gulls' eggs is illegal, but Mr Dey maintained that it was 'estate practice' in order to cut down on the number of birds eating grouse eggs. Asked if the estate turned a bind eye to such thefts, he replied: 'Let's just say that, if there are no grouse or pheasants, there are no jobs for the keepers.' A member of the Royal Society for the Protection of Birds mentioned other alleged incidents on the estate involving the persecution of wildlife.

There is little doubt that the modern Seafield estate is no longer the traditional, paternalistic property which it may have been 40 years ago under the late Countess of Seafield, who was widely known as one of Britain's largest landowners and wealthiest women. The estate has contracted in size, it is managed on a day-to-day basis by a factor who is described as gruff or 'never wrong', and, it is said, difficult to deal with.

It has, for example, been less than helpful to Scottish Natural Heritage, the environment agency, at its Aviemore headquarters. The organisation owns the building which it occupies and successfully applied for planning permission to add an extension. Seafield, although no longer the owner of the site, was still the feudal superior and tried to block the extension.

It is also said to use this anachronistic position as feudal superior to extract payments whenever possible from tenants, owners of former Seafield land and local businesses seeking to expand.

There was a similar tale from estate tenants in tied properties on the Cullen coast who were asked in the 1980s to make a payment to allow them to remain in their homes. 'They make sure they get all they can from their feudal rights,' said one Grantown conservationist.

A member of SNH said of the estate's management ethos: 'It is run as a business which does not take on board the importance of the local community or the environment. It is being pared down all the time. Not so long ago it employed its own foresters and nurserymen, now work is contracted from the outside.'

He was also highly critical of the scarring caused by bulldozed roads which were carved out on the Kinveachy sporting estate to provide access to potentially lucrative grouse-shooting. 'It is a crime ecologically and economically. It makes no sense.'

And he suggested that efforts by the estate to reduce red deer numbers had been 'half-hearted'. Deer reductions are required under the Woodland Grant Schemes – to extend or enhance native forests – which the estate has adopted in return for substantial grants from the Forestry Commission.

Sport – principally salmon-fishing on the rich River Spey, deerstalking and grouse-shooting – is the main economic support, with forestry and farming completing the picture. The involvement in native woodland schemes reflects the estate's long interest in forestry. It was the late countess who was credited with retaining the Abernethy Caledonian pine forest in reasonable condition before that area was sold to the RSPB. Yet in modern times, forestry has proved to be another sore point for tenants. In 1995, the factor wrote to farm tenants following the designation of some of the estate lands as part of the new Cairngorms Environmentally Sensitive Area. ESAs cover just over 15 per cent of Scotland and are an almost universally welcomed designation because they provide payments for farmers in return for conservation works.

Therefore, the scheme offers a subsidy which can both enhance habitats while at the same time rewarding farmers for improving the health of their land rather – as so many subsidies did in the past – than rewarding them for damaging the land. Of particular interest to the farming tenants were the payments available for the improvement of areas of native woodland, through fencing and complete or partial stock removal. Removing sheep at the right time of year would help the regeneration of natural woodland.

The factor, however, wrote to tenants, essentially warning them that if they entered into the ESA scheme they could be held to be in breach of their tenancy, which states they must use the land for agricultural purposes. Any improved woodland on farmland, it was suggested, would be resumed by the estate – which, of course, could claim substantial grants by entering the 'new' woodland into a different environment scheme, for example, the WGS scheme offered by the Forestry Commission.

The exact motive of the estate is difficult to establish without an explanation, but from outside – and, indeed, to the tenants – it looked like nothing more than envy and greed. Paternalistic, it was not.

One tenant who received the letter explained: 'Trees normally belong to the estate, so it was not normally in the interest of the farmers to grow trees. The ESA would provide financial benefits to farmers. On the other hand, the Woodland Grant Scheme figures are very generous and if the estate had taken back areas of woodland and entered them into that scheme it could have done quite well. People have grown to expect these sort of things from estates, it is an endless conflict.'

There also was a suggestion, at least in the minds of tenants, that their rents would be reviewed upwards if they entered the ESA.

Such obstruction, of course, is completely counter to the ethos of the scheme which is intended to benefit people working on the land and enhance the environment. Seafield's reluctance to welcome the designation is in contrast to the approach of some other properties. On one estate run by the Crown Estate commission – whose profits support the Civil List – tenants are positively encouraged to enter the scheme.

Eventually, the dispute was resolved when the factor appeared to alter his stance on the issue and withdrew his objections. Although, at the time of writing, no one could name a farmer who had applied to join the ESA.

According to another farmer, tenants themselves are becoming an endangered breed. He saw the biggest problem on the modern Seafield estates to be the trend towards depopulation of the countryside. He explained what was happening this way: 'There is a pattern of selling the assets. If the estate is selling land, it is much more valuable if the farm is in partnership and is not under tenancy. There is no security of tenure in a partnership.

'So if a farmer dies or somebody does not want to take up a tenancy, the estate takes it back. They will put the poor ground under one of the forestry schemes to get grants, and lump the rest of the land in with another farm. The population is declining, that is our biggest fear.'

According to the farmer, the land might be worth only half as much if it was sold with a farm tenant enjoying security of tenure. The change also provides an opportunity to sell steadings for development. Partnerships between the estate and the tenant will typically last for only five or ten years.

Another business with complaints to make is the Strathspey Railway Company, which runs a steam train from Aviemore to Boat of Garten. It has had numerous problems, including some difficulties over its plan to extend the railway to Grantown-on-Spey; the estate claimed it owned part of the land on the route and, according to one source, 'was bloody-minded in the hope of getting some money'.

One concerned businessman went so far as to predict a mass vote for the Scottish National Party because of its pledge to reform the feudal system. The same man asked me: 'Have you found that all big estates are like this?' Well, no.

There are numerous other tales told of rows with local salmon anglers, of a restaurant owner asked for a one-off payment by the feudal superior, of a farmer being given short notice to quit and of former agricultural land being ploughed up and planted for forestry – all instances which have been chewed over by the locals and repeated, no doubt, many times.

Even an individual who has had a lengthy association with the estate barely gave it the benefit of the doubt. He said: 'Obviously the estate has got to pay its way in a competitive world and take opportunities when it sees them and look after its own interests where it can. That is quite normal, although I can see it may not be very popular in the eyes of the local community.' A few decades ago, he suggested, the estate was very much the guardian and provider in the same community and supported in some way 'just about every local organisation'. 'Now it tends to be run by people with no ties with the community and undoubtedly it has changed for the worse.'

It was not all bad, he insisted. He quoted the example of new paths and cycle tracks – 'a very large scheme' – in woodland between Grantown and Aviemore, without the carrot of grants and profit.

Seafield is in some senses an example of a trend which is more or less visible on a number of Highland estates which have been put into trust and which are trying, by more businesslike methods (and rarely succeeding), to make some profit, any profit. Something similar was happening on the Invercauld estate of Capt. Alwyn Farquharson, where a trust was attempting to put the vast property on a commercial footing, and irritating some of the gamekeepers employed there in the process.

With hindsight, it may be possible to say that these estates were trying the impossible; that they could not make a reasonable profit from the traditional land uses, with the subsidies available. Perhaps they are great big monuments to the unworkability of the Common Agricultural Policy, the too many decades of extractive sporting regimes and the reliance on a feudal system which had had its time.

Is Seafield one of the worst estates in Scotland? Certainly, it is highly unpopular, but there may be others which are little known outside a small locality and which have a far better claim to such a title. One contender would be the central Scotland estate of Blackford. Stretching to around 20,000 acres, it was bought in the 1970s by His Excellency Mahdi Mohammed Al Tajir, formerly the ambassador to Britain of the United Arab Emirates, and an individual who once claimed to be the wealthiest man in the world.

The estate is made up of fertile ground between Dunblane and Gleneagles. Over a period of 20 years, when tenant farmers retired or left the estate, the mainly absent owner developed a habit of leaving houses derelict, while the land (more recently) was increasingly entered into the Set Aside scheme which pays owners to take land out of production. The result is a rabbit-ridden landscape dotted with more than 20 derelict and decaying homes.

The estate was featured on the BBC's *Frontline Scotland* programme in which tenant farmer George Mitchell commented: 'I felt very angry that a foreign owner could come and say to a Scotsman that he cannot live in Scotland.' Mr Mitchell tried to buy his late father's farmhouse from the estate, but was refused permission on the basis that only members of the owner's family should live within its boundaries!

The positive aspect of the ownership is said to be the fact that one of Britain's most popular mineral waters, Highland Spring, is bottled in Blackford and provides 130 jobs. The estate claims it has to keep the land free of unwanted development – including farming – in order to maintain the purity of the water. The statement makes very little ecological sense, and the system of management on Blackford has even been criticised by the Scottish Landowners' Federation. Perhaps in very different estates like Seafield and Blackford, there will be found the beginnings of a revolt by traditionally conservative tenants which will fuel long-overdue reform.

LAND USE ON THE ESTATES

	ASSYNT	LETTEREWE	MAR LODGE	BUCCLEUCH	ATHOLL	LOCHIEL	S. UIST	ALCAN	SUTHERLAND	SEAFIELD
Absent, or partly absent, owner	◆	◆		◆	◆	◆	◆			
Managed mainly by factor	◆	◆	◆		◆	◆	◆	◆		◆
Little or no natural regeneration	◆	◆	◆	◆	◆	◆	◆	◆	◆	◆
Only limited jobs provider	◆	◆		◆	◆	◆			◆	
On-going or past loss of heather moor	◆	◆	◆	◆	◆	◆	◆	◆	◆	◆
Linked now or in past with raptor persecution	◆		◆	◆	◆		◆		◆	◆
Lower game bags than past	◆	◆	◆	◆	◆	◆	◆	◆	◆	◆
Owner seen as remote or unpopular	◆									◆
Fails to make regular profit	◆	◆	◆		◆	◆		◆		
Suffers from over-grazing	◆	◆	◆	◆	◆	◆	◆	◆	◆	◆

CONCLUSION

A Time for Change

'Private landowners can be expected to resist the necessary legislation, but not too fiercely. However, when it comes to administering my final prescription, the nationalisation of all land, the fun will begin.'

John McEwen, *Who Owns Scotland?*

One of the landowners interviewed by me posed the question: what would you do if, by accident of birth, you found that you owned a large area of land? Would you sell it off and live comfortably on the proceeds? Or would you be bound by a sense of responsibility, and try to maintain and manage the land as best you could? That, he said, was the question critics must ask themselves.

The point was well made. It is very easy from outside the apparently cosy coterie of landowners in Scotland, to criticise the system and suggest there is a better way. The Dutch landowner who made the point no doubt was identifying the basic sense of responsibility which comes with any inheritance – or even purchase – be it a silver spoon or a deer forest in the Highlands.

My prime purpose is not to criticise the actions of individuals who may understandably want to work the land as their fathers did before them, but to question a system which on many fronts can be said to have failed the vast majority of Scots.

There is unease with the degraded state of the natural environment of much of the upland estate, and there is a growing belief that the land could be more productive, and could contribute more to local communities.

There is understandable unease, at the beginning of the new millennium, with the outdated feudal system. It is wrong that a feudal superior – normally a major landowner – can continue to influence the development of a property owned by someone else. A home owner on Atholl estate, for example, has to ask for permission from the 'superior' in order to extend 'his' property, or to start a business.

There are concerns also about the lack of local benefit accruing from other owners of our land. From the Forestry Commission woodlands, from the croftlands owned by the Scottish Executive Agriculture, Environment and Fisheries department, and from the seabed around small coastal communities which is owned by the Crown Estate Commission. Seabed rents from fish farms, for example, help support the royal family.

In such a climate it is surely remarkable that an outdated, outmoded and unloved land-owning system remains stubbornly a part of Scotland's furniture, not much different from the way it was in the late 1970s – those last of the socialist times – when John McEwen wrote *Who Owns Scotland?*, when there was just a chance for radical change. The Labour Party, under Jim Callaghan's Government, had a policy of land nationalisation, and the young Gordon Brown was a strong supporter of McEwen, the arch critic of the lairds. The Scottish national Party enjoyed a historic high with 13 MPs, and the 7:84 Company, which owed its very name to the injustice of land-ownership concentrated in the hands of the few, rammed home these issues to its lively audiences.

Yet by the time the Conservatives won the 1979 general election, the 'Scottish issue' was already off the political agenda. And in the ensuing years, the widening gap in understanding between urban and rural populations has, if anything, helped private ownership to thrive. Although many resent the idea of large-scale land-ownership, the public today tend to have less knowledge than ever of country life, and therefore less ability to criticise it usefully.

There remain around 4,000 members of the Scottish Landowners' Federation who own around seven million acres, or 80 per cent of Scotland. So has anything changed?

As the 400 mourners filed quietly from St Mary's Church, following the lone piper and the eight pall-bearers, it was tempting to see something deeply symbolic in what was happening. This was the funeral of the popular clan chief and war hero, Lord 'Shimi' Lovat. But was it also a funeral for land-owning itself?

Lord Lovat died in March 1994, aged 83, having lived a remarkable life. He died at a time of tragedy for his family, one year after the deaths of two of his sons, and after witnessing the decline of the family fortune and the estate lands centred at Beaufort Castle on the edge of Beauly.

His son, Simon, the former Master of Lovat, had squandered estate money on a series of unsuccessful ventures, and died leaving debts of £7.4 million. There is nothing remarkable about this in the history of the great families: much the same happened on the Breadalbane and Sutherland lands, in Atholl and Tongue and elsewhere. But here was one of the great families losing its grip and one of the great estates crumbling away.

All three Lovat funerals were held at St Mary's Church, at Eskdale, above the black River Beauly. On the day of Lord Lovat's funeral, the Beauly itself was part of the story: the entire river system was sold to the highest bidder by the Master of Lovat during troubled times, and much against the wishes of Lord Lovat.

The slide from great fortune was visible as the funeral ended. The new Lord Lovat, 18-year-old Simon Fraser, then a Harrow schoolboy, left the church in a battered Subaru estate. Months later the estate ground and the castle were sold in 39 lots.

In death, Lord Lovat was remembered not as a disappointed old man who had seen his son all but destroy that which successive generations had sought to preserve, but as the brave character who led his troops on to Sword Beach on D-Day, with piper Bill Millin at his side. And, as the mourners filed away to a reception at the castle, and with the snow trying to fall, Piper Bill stood alone at the graveside and played three tunes for his old friend, laments for a popular clan chief.

In some regard, these were also laments for a way of life. There is little prospect of the family regaining the 140,000 acres lost over the decades.

Other estates have been lost in the same way and other mourners at the funeral had seen their own lands diminished. They included Cameron of Lochiel and Lord Strathnaver of the Sutherland estates.

Sir Donald Cameron was wearing the Jacobite colours which were once worn by his ancestor under the hopeless banner of Prince Charles Edward Stuart. He remains a clan chief, but one who looks to Camerons around the world for money to retain the clan museum, while the family estate faces an uncertain future.

This funeral happened at a time when the first shoots of a renewed interest in the issue of land-owning were reappearing. As I write this, *The Scotsman* and *Scotland on Sunday* newspapers are reporting regularly on matters of the land.

One article in *Scotland on Sunday* sticks in my mind. It detailed the revival in the fortunes of Ben Alder estate, which had been taken over by a millionaire Swiss intent on creating a dream mansion on the shores of cold Loch Ericht. By building a magnificent occasional home, he was displaying the kind of disposable income no longer available to the Fraser family. The contrast with the down-at-heel Scottish gentry could not have been greater. The same is true of numerous overseas owners: Count Knuth, for example, the Danish aristocratic owner of Ben Loyal estate in the north of Scotland, who won an architectural award for his restoration of, of all things, a boathouse.

Scotland's big freshwater lochs are littered with boathouses in disrepair – mini-monuments to the death of conspicuous landed wealth.

So here, within a matter of weeks, were two clear strands in the modern development of land-owning. On the one hand the ongoing, seemingly inevitable, decline and fall of the old families, on the other hand the arrival of Scotland's new multi-millionaire businessmen, the van Vlissingens and the Al Fayeds. And, in the case of the Lovat estate, the new rich in the shape of Mrs Ann Gloag, the bus conductor's daughter from Perth who was the co-founder of the Stagecoach bus company. In August 1995, she bought Beaufort Castle for £1.3 million. Her granny, she said, had been a Fraser.

Is the future so simple? Will the old families simply die out and squander their money (through the folly of Young Lochinvar), and will the techno-millionaires, foreign investors seeking tax breaks and the nouveau riche move in to claim the hills?

This is not just a scenario. It is happening at the moment and the trend has been gathering since the 1970s. This process (and even the alternative of estates being handed from generation to generation) is objectionable for the simple fact that there must be a better way – as there is in Scandinavia, in Denmark, in the Netherlands, in Switzerland, and in so many other countries where there are restrictions on who can buy land and what can be done with it.

In some parts of Holland, only local residents are allowed to buy houses for sale in order to stop them being purchased by absentees from Amsterdam (the same system would serve well in Braemar); in Denmark there is a regulation which prevents foreigners – specifically Germans – from buying land; in Norway, the purchaser of a farm must promise to live on it for five years and must manage it in the approved way. None of this is called xenophobia, just simple common sense, or stewardship of the land.

In Scotland, the system of ownership is not the result of years of integrated planning and land-use reform. It is an anachronism, partly retained by the influence of those holding land, partly by the acquiescence of successive governments, and partly by the indifference of the bulk of the Scottish population.

What are the results of such slack governance? The answer lies most importantly in the inflated value of marginal hill land in the Highlands. As long as Scottish land – never mind the entirely non-ecological and entirely unnatural delimitation of the estate boundary – is available on the world market to the highest bidder, then land will have value which it does not deserve in agricultural terms, and which removes it from the reach of ordinary people and communities.

There are, of course, enlightened, intelligent and concerned overseas landowners in Scotland. Yet they may buy land first and foremost because of their own fascination with the Scottish landscape, because of their love of wild places and the feeling of wilderness which is lacking, yet so appealing, in their business lives. It may be something to do with a love of the sports of deerstalking and fishing, but it will not often be about the improvement of the local community, about the establishment or encouragement of new enterprise, or the enhancement of endangered habitats. And it is very unlikely to be about getting more people into the countryside and stopping the drift towards urban areas which can be seen in most remote Scottish communities.

In this, the landowners are guilty of nothing more than human nature. Just as it is human nature for such powerful individuals to be confident they will be good for the land, and for the community. That they will be 'good absentee landowners'. Indeed, the best absentee landowner can be a lot better than the worst resident owner, but he cannot be very much more if he is out of touch with Scottish politics and the evolving debates on rural land-use. Most of the landowners featured here, it should be said, are far from the worst.

Happily, the pattern of land-owning in Scotland is changing, and this mix is broadening. For the first time, charitable trusts concerned about environmental issues are buying land. Environment groups, boosted by the money available from the National Lottery, are increasingly adding to their own portfolios. The National Trust for Scotland bought Mar Lodge estate in the Cairngorms, and organisations such as the John Muir Trust and the Royal Society for the Protection of Birds are leading the way elsewhere, with the environment at the top of the agenda. And, if you can believe the selling agents, there is a new enlightened 'family' man moving into ownership, as much interested in the sundew and the twinflower as the twin-barrel and the grouse.

But whatever changes are taking place – and an increasing mix of ownership types is to be welcomed – it is not a comprehensive change, and the open market remains open to abuse. There are no guarantees when Scottish land is bought and sold.

Yet there is increasing public concern about the amount of land in offshore companies and foreign hands – certainly more than 500,000 acres. I was astonished to be told by a former director of the Scottish Landowners' Federation that he had 'no feeling' about how much land was owned by overseas interests.

The island of Eigg in the Inner Hebrides, for example, had been sold for around £1.5 million by the unpopular Yorkshireman Keith Schellenberg to the German spiritual artist Professor Marlin Maruma. Schellenberg left the island as an enemy of the 80-strong population, his vintage Rolls-Royce destroyed in a mysterious fire. At one point he called the islanders 'hippies' and hooligans, and they said 'good riddance'. Private ownership at less than its best.

In his place, the islanders got the 'millionaire painter' – apparently unknown in his own country – who first saw Eigg on a glorious August day in 1994 and decided, on impulse, to buy it, instead of an island in the Seychelles. The decision came to him while he stood in an old cave which had witnessed the massacre of 600 islanders, deliberately imprisoned and burned to death, in the ancient warring history of the Hebridean clans.

It was only after his inevitable financial failure – he promised to spend millions of pounds which he did not have – that the island was put back on the market and the islanders succeeded, with the aid of popular donations, in buying their land.

Knoydart is another example. The whole, square, hauntingly rugged peninsula was once a single entity. It was bought and deliberately broken up over the years by an English property developer. The 17,000-acre core which was left was finally purchased by the Dundee jute company, Titaghur. The chairman wanted to create an outward-bound centre for problem youngsters in the lodge on Knoydart, but that was a year before his company fell £60 million into debt and he faced allegations of fraud and the issue of a warrant for his arrest by Interpol. After another period of farcical ownership, in 1999 the estate finally became the property of the locals and could become one of the most exciting community ownership projects in Scotland.

Then there was Strathconon estate, a chunk of 60,000 acres which was sold for around £2 million to the Danish owners of the Lego toy company; Lego would have been unable to buy land in Denmark as a result of a 1973 Act which prevents the purchase of property for 'recreation or hobby-farming' uses.

No such concerns in Scotland.

The system of land management as practised by private owners can be criticised, with ease, from an environmental perspective. Perhaps the most important question to ask is simply this: what should we, the public, demand from the land?

Here are two possible answers.

1. If the answer is the continuation of the current regime dominated by sporting use, and driven largely by personal motivation and the entirely unco-ordinated, short-term subsidies for agriculture, forestry and commercial development, then nothing need be done. We would have to accept, however, that in many areas a continuation on current lines would also mean a slow but steady loss of health on the land. Perhaps we would simply like to have a register of land-ownership set up, so that at least we would have the satisfaction of knowing who owned what, and how much it was worth in Hong Kong.

2. If we start accepting that much of rural Scotland, in the big Borders hill farm estates as well as on the moor and grass hills of the Highlands, is performing way below its biological potential – both because of the sporting interests and inappropriate agriculture subsidies to estate tenants – then we must seek radical change.

Do we want Scotland's 'poorer' land to perform nearer to its potential in terms of production, and do we want to see more people living in the countryside? Do we want the natural resources on which any sustainable future for the Highlands must be based, to be distributed more equitably?

If the answer is yes, then do we have the scientific evidence to support our arguments?

The celebrated, misunderstood and oft-ignored-by-the-establishment naturalist, Frank Fraser Darling, recognised many of the great problems of the Highland lands between the 1930s and '60s. He was commissioned by the Scottish Office in the 1940s to write the 'West Highland Survey', which documented his ideas on problems and solutions for human ecology. He did not even receive an acknowledgement from the Scottish Office when he submitted the report.

In the 1960s, in the conclusion to his book, *Natural History in the Highlands and Islands*, written with John Morton Boyd, he observed: 'The greatest strength of any countryside is preservation of maximum natural variety.'

At the time he welcomed the establishment of the Nature Conservancy Council (now Scottish Natural Heritage), the freshwater fisheries laboratories at Pitlochry and the purchase of some important mountain estates by the NCC for conservation reasons. In his time he also saw the Labour Government's Highlands and Islands Development Board as the kernel of change in the land tenure system. He realised there was much to be done.

'Unfortunately,' he wrote, 'there is still evident administratively the neat notion of efficiency which leads away from maintenance of the varied habitat towards a simple monocultural one.'

The Highlands, he said, had become a devastated terrain which political and administrative acts could not restore without biological understanding. He remarked: 'This was a most unpopular opinion to express in the 1940s, and even now has scarcely penetrated St Andrew's House.' Had he been alive today, he would not rewrite that last sentence. Decisions taken today by politicians, and advice given by civil servants, seem still to exhibit no true understanding of the fundamental needs and threats facing many of Scotland's precious habitats. The Scottish Executive is, at last, addressing land reform, but we have heard little from it on the subject of the natural environment. The quite naturally interlinked businesses of farming, forestry, fishing and country sports are still run entirely separately, with no integrated planning, no overview of what is happening to the land.

Fraser Darling was convinced of the need for more research, and much work has been done. Imagine, however, that it was only in 1995 that detailed efforts were being made by the Macaulay Land Use Research Institute in Aberdeen, the Institute of Terrestrial Ecology and SNH to understand the dynamics of the relationship between deer and its habitat, in order to establish the carrying capacity of the land.

Meanwhile, research on heather moorland in Scotland has shown it is in decline for a variety of reasons. These include grazing pressure by sheep and deer, bad burning practice carried out to provide new growth for sheep or grouse, and acidic deposition caused by industrial pollution and car exhausts.

On an area like Glenfeshie in the Cairngorms, bought by the charity Will Woodlands in 1994 and by a Danish millionaire in 1997, the effects of deer damage are startlingly obvious.

The heather is cropped indecently short, areas of moorland are turning to grass under pressure of the herds and there are clear signs of serious erosion on the steep flanks of the glen. There are blocks of plantation forestry, some of it planted underneath the old pine trees of Caledon; and to make matters worse, the exotic trees were introduced with the now-discredited downhill ploughing which allows fast drainage of the water and the loss of silt and nutrients. The damage to the environment is more obvious here than in any other core Cairngorms estate, including Mar Lodge.

Will Woodlands had no track record of managing mountain estates, and singularly failed during its short period of ownership to bring about the Mar Lodge-style deer cull necessary on the ravaged land. When it put the estate back on the market it was, once again, whipped away from conservation hands by foreign money, this time in the shape of Danish clothes designer Klaus Helmerson.

There is ample scientific concern today, echoing, 50 years on, the words of Fraser Darling. In *Scotland – Land of Mountains*, published in October 1995 by photographer Colin Baxter, SNH scientist Des Thompson lamented: 'I am repeatedly disappointed by the poor stature of our vegetation, and the many signs of heavy grazing, burning and erosion.

'In many parts the exposure of rocks, screes and bare ground is greater than would have been seen in earlier centuries, and this seems to stem from the stripping away of plant life and associated soil processes. Only a few centimetres of soil and plants may separate the bedrock from the elements of nature. Yet we take this for granted and seem surprised when the land fails the fertility test and gradually loses its plant cover.'

He believes that much could be done, partly through the improvement and further designation of Environmentally Sensitive Areas – an EU mechanism which allows payments to farmers for positive conservation management and which currently captures just over 15 per cent of Scotland. He believes moss, lichen and dwarf shrub cover should be restored on the mountain tops, and that dwarf herbs, juniper, willow and birch could thrive again at their upper altitudinal limit.

'There is a richness and diversity in this landscape of mountains – from rolling hills to rugged peaks, steep glens to mountain lochs and from the land to the sea with its many islands. Yet we have lost our trees, many of our heaths and smothered some of our greatest bogs with plantations. Stony heaps and old "lazy" beds mark the eviction of a people and the loss of a culture once married to the land. Sheep and deer now roam the hill, their numbers often out of kilter with habitats on which they depend. Bulldozed tracks, ragged paths and contemporary artifacts breach and scar the wild tops – helping some but offending others.'

The critics may look at such statements and ask, what has this got to do with estate management and with social benefits in a marginal rural community? Such a question indicates not just a lack of spiritual appreciation of nature and hill land, but also an ignorance of 'whole habitats' and the benefits – social as well as environmental – which can accrue from them.

Thompson concludes: 'Many regions of the world have sacred and mystical elements of nature associated with their mountains. There, one finds degrees of reverence and protection not found in Scotland. Our mountains have an aura of spirituality, but not a corresponding degree of sanctity. The mountains deserve our best.'

In his emotive pamphlet *Ill Fares the Land*, Sir John Lister-Kaye, the former chairman of the north-west board of SNH, and a landowner himself, decries the craziness of much of the sporting estate system. Rain, wrote Lister-Kaye, should filter through bogs, heather, scrub and woodland 'to emerge as a nutritious soup' on which the whole of the freshwater system is based.

There is ample research to show that the freshwater system in Scotland, our precious lochs and rivers, so closely associated with the undeserved 'pure' image of the country, have long been in decline. Any landowner who has been around more than a few decades will tell you tales of the trout he used to catch, of the large salmon regularly taken from the river. One of our greatest naturalists, Seton Gordon, wrote of toiling uphill with salmon slung from his bicycle from a glen river which today yields less in a year than it formerly did in a week.

The fact that salmon are in decline is no doubt due to a plethora of reasons, including high-seas fishing and coastal drift-netting, but there is also clear evidence that many river systems in Scotland are suffering through lack of management – particularly on the vital higher reaches where the salmon spawn, where the landowner gets nothing in the way of rent for salmon-fishing (unlike his downstream neighbours), and where next to no maintenance of the river is done. Man's actions, whether damming for hydro-power, keeping livestock on the bank – which can lead to erosion – or simply failing to clear obstructions caused, perhaps, by flash floods induced by the lack of vegetation on hillsides, has damaged these vital grounds, but not beyond repair.

The problem in the river systems, and in many natural systems, is, again, the lack of strategic, integrated management of the resource: most rivers are managed selfishly in compartments – as if the human might opt to look after just one part of his or her body and expect the rest to function well.

So it is with sporting estates. The land is managed for deer and grouse and salmon and not for the lungs – the intact vegetation – or for the flesh and the bones – the soil on which everything must be based.

Wildlife itself is a resource under threat, as revealed in a report published by SNH on the state of Scotland's natural heritage. Due to its lack of true independence from Government or Treasury purse strings, SNH couched this 1995 study in very careful (bland) language, which might give the casual reader the impression that Scotland was a treasure trove of natural wonders. At a glance, however, the tables contained in the document tell a very different story. (Here, of course, is a story in its own right. A so-called independent government agency struggling to produce a statement on environmental health which, if poor, would reflect badly on its paymaster – the then Scottish Office!)

The tables revealed that of the 48 land mammals in Scotland, a total of 12 are known to be in decline, and the status of several others is uncertain. And, with the exception of the pine marten, only those animals closely associated with significant environmental damage were on the increase – specifically deer, rabbits and grey seals. The document listed many bird species in serious decline, the loss of 30 flowering plants since the 1930s and the disappearance of 26 mosses and lichens.

While many species have declined due to loss of habitat, others are still being damaged by illegal persecution carried out by gamekeepers on sporting estates, while the owner turns a blind eye. When a keeper is caught and appears in court for killing a golden eagle or a peregrine falcon, for example, the owner invariably avows his innocence, protesting that he had 'no idea' what was happening. In reality, this is likely to be disingenuous. It is the laird who will tell his keeper that the grouse numbers must improve next year, or that the shoot must not be disturbed by a peregrine falcon swooping across the moor.

There are a number of estates where illegal killing of birds of prey is known to go on, and those estates which are caught are certainly the tip of the iceberg. In 1994, the RSPB recorded nearly 400 incidents of persecution in Scotland. And in 1999, landowners called for the killing of birds of prey to be approved by the Scottish Secretary in order to protect grouse numbers – ignoring both the advice that raptor populations are only beginning to recover after years of persecution and pollution, and the suggestion from scientists that better land management is the answer to healthier grouse moors.

Similarly, landowners increasingly complain about the number of badgers – 'there has been an explosion in the south-west', I was told – and about the recovery of the pine marten. Both species are certain already to be the subject of some illegal persecution.

So far, I have concentrated on the environmental imperatives which point to a time for change. Other commentators will deal more wisely with social questions.

However, as I have suggested, there is often an overlap in environmental and community interests. A visit to Norway, for example, would suggest that where semi-natural habitats are flourishing, so there are more opportunities for local people. Particularly when the habitat is the subject of community ownership: orchards provide fruit, timber comes from the woodlands and is milled locally, and craft and tourism industries are greatly enhanced. The near-natural environment supports more wildlife and more opportunities in game or sporting revenue. I will return to the Norwegian example later.

One of the key proponents of land reform in Scotland is the writer and historian Dr James Hunter, the author of several books on the Highland condition. On 22 September 1995, the third anniversary of the death of John McEwen, he delivered a lecture in Dingwall which was an important new marker in the land-owning debate.

He called for the eradication of feudalism and for all crofting lands, whether owned by lairds or by the Scottish Office agriculture department, to be returned to crofters. (Feudalism, lest we forget the underpinning absurdity of the current system, allowed, in 1995, the English company which owns the Rosehaugh estate on the Black Isle to demand compensation for the sale of houses no longer in its possession. As feudal superior, it could continue to make demands on property it had long since sold.)

Dr Hunter's main proposal was that Scotland's crofting landlords – across one million acres – could be bought out for around £10 million, on the basis of the existing mechanism which allows crofters to buy their land for as little as 15 times the annual rent. This formula applies to inbye land next to the croft and may produce a purchase cost of no more than £450 per croft. Controversially, Hunter suggested applying the formula to the common grazing, an idea which, if followed through, would result in landowners receiving compensation for their land at well below international market values.

In addition, he called for coastal communities to be given responsibility for the management of the seabed and the foreshore – it is currently owned and managed by the Crown Estate Commissioners for the benefit of the Civil List – for farming tenants to become owners of their farms, and for the Forestry Commission to make plantations available to local interests.

He also recognised some inertia in the crofting communities by suggesting that crofters should be obliged to become more involved in the running of their affairs: community ownership would be forced on them.

His key message was that land reform was neither impractical nor prohibitively expensive. 'Reform,' he said, 'can be justified – legally, morally, socially, economically – if it is forward-looking; if it is meant to empower and liberate; if it is intended to promote new forms of development; if it is not undertaken merely in some spirit of revenge for crimes committed long ago.'

Hunter believes radical land reform should be a first priority for the Scottish Parliament, a test of its integrity, although he recognises that politicians cannot always be relied upon to grasp unpopular policies, even when they are for the greater good. With the necessary political will, he suggested, the crofting landlord of the Highlands could be consigned to history on 1 January in the year 2000.

But Dr Hunter's ideas are, for the moment, too radical. The Scottish Executive missed its millennial deadline by opting for a programme of land reform that adds up to no more than the early steps necessary to bring about significant changes in our countryside. On the other hand, John McEwen's demand for nationalisation of land was going too far.

Certainly, whoever the owner, there is room for more prescription in how our land is used, and there is considerable room for development through the revision of the hopelessly clumsy Common Agricultural Policy and the redirection of subsidies and grants to provide social and environmental benefits. Where one exists without the other, you end up, for example, with the sheep subsidy which keeps hills overstocked, men on the land and the land in decline.

The EU also spends around £800 million on the lunacy of 'set aside' – much of it going to large landowners – which provides payments to take fields out of agriculture, while offering little incentive for positive management of the surplus areas created. One Arab owner in central Scotland receives £200,000 a year from the CAP for leaving his fields derelict and unworked.

Yet the right subsidies are, of course, vital in the Highlands and other marginal areas. Professor Bryan MacGregor, of the department of land economy at Aberdeen University, put this neatly when he told me: 'Subsidies are the wrong word. We pay for what we consume in the Highlands: the solitude, the beauty, the environment. We want those areas to look like they do. The people who live there provide us with that. It is not so much a subsidy, as the price we pay as individuals to consume these areas.'

In order to have something infinitely better to consume, we need to create a system in which it is the capacity of the land itself to support produce and support people, in a sustainable fashion, which determines the management of our uplands and glens and straths. Subsidies should not be paid on the basis of the 'headage' system in which money is paid for the number of sheep, the acres of grain and even, under Set Aside, for the acres not producing.

Positive change may be achieved by stricter control over who owns what and how it is managed, but it will also require radical changes in the way that statutory agencies and legislation influence land management.

In simple terms, there needs to be more regulation and less reliance on the voluntary principle. Subsidies should be tailored for the Highland physical and human environment. These would encourage the restoration of mixed, natural forest cover in many areas, a reduction in the number of sheep on the hills, a contraction of the area of land dedicated to open-hill deerstalking and grouse-shooting, and support for community ownership of land, woods and shores. Something approximating to the Norwegian situation.

Modern Norway, in an area like Hordaland on the west coast, was created in little more than a century, and is now a relatively prosperous community. Norwegian governments have always accepted that a stable population in even the furthest-flung rural areas is an important social goal, and have subsidised communities hundreds of miles inside the Arctic Circle, even on the beautiful, but agriculturally challenged, Lofoten Islands.

Hordaland has many similarities with areas of Scotland – it has a high rainfall, an oceanic boreal ecology, a glacially eroded plateau and it is dependent on natural resources. Land is mainly privately owned, but mostly by small families. If a farm is sold to an outsider, that person must be assessed to establish his suitability, and must agree to live on and operate the property for at least five years.

The average holding is ten hectares of farmland and 56 hectares of forest, although farm sizes are becoming larger under outside economic influences. Highland region has twice the land area of Hordaland and less than half the population. In Norway, the level of subsidy is higher, but is properly concentrated on small farms, while the majority of EU subsidies in Britain go to the largest 10 per cent of the land managers. Agricultural wages in Norway are deliberately kept as near industrial level as possible. And no less than 50 per cent of the forestry is owned by the farmers.

The nub of it is this, that much of the 'marginal' land in Norway is forested and managed in a way that at least approaches its productive potential and contributes to the support of a significant human population. The land use is sustainable.

In Scotland, much of the land is deforested, in active degradation, suffering declining productivity, diversity and gradual loss of wildlife, scenic and amenity value. The land cannot sustain, in the very long term, the uses to which it is predominantly subjected.

When a group of farmers, foresters, councillors and environmentalists returned from a Scottish study tour of Norway they brought with them wild imaginings of apple and cherry orchards in the west Highlands, fruit gardens on Skye. After all, if Osgood Mackenzie could do it with a barren peninsula at Poolewe, why could not the same be achieved on a much grander scale?

The lessons learned were best summed up by Angus McHattie of the Scottish Crofters' Union who, back home on Skye, was moved to write: 'On returning to Skye recently I had occasion to compare the view from similar 3,000ft granite hills in both countries. In Norway, the valley I looked down upon contained an autonomous village of 20 small farms, with their own crops, power supply, school, et cetera – a prosperous and happy place with a good trade surplus and a population with a healthy age structure

'The Skye valley had 20 black-faced ewes and 12 lambs. Compared to what the Norwegians started with, we are sitting on a gold mine. The development potential of the Highlands and Islands is immense.'

It will be many years, generations perhaps, before we see the over-used landscape of Skye looking like a Norwegian valley. But the change of government in 1997 has made improvements more likely.

Ewen Cameron, a historian at Edinburgh University, said the Scottish Executive's land reform legislation added up to 'the pursuit of what is less disruptive, the minimum possible reform to retain support and to argue that promises have been fulfilled whilst alienating the fewest'.

Given the nature of real politics, this may be a little harsh, although Andy Wightman, the land reform campaigner, goes further. In a newspaper article in 1999, he pointed out that Scotland had the most concentrated pattern of private land ownership in the world, with just 343 lairds owning over half the privately owned rural land.

Wightman could see no revolution on the horizon. Rather, the abolition of feudalism 'will have no impact on the situation', and the legislation giving communities the right to buy land when it comes on the market will 'dismally fail to achieve the government's objectives either of empowering communities or effecting a rapid change in the pattern of land ownership'. He suggests that measures that would make this happen include giving legal rights to children to inherit land, placing limits on the size of holdings and giving tenant farmers the right to buy their farms. Other radical changes might involve abolishing offshore titles and making landowners live on their land.

In the early stages of the reform plans, there was a proposal to allow tenant farmers to buy their land. Such a move might have led, of course, to the fragmentation of some big estates, and was therefore strongly opposed by the lairds.

Remarkably, when the final details of the land reform Bill were announced in Edinburgh, there was little dissension from the landowners who attended the historic occasion. Indeed, the Duke of Buccleuch told me afterwards that there was nothing in the proposals that caused him undue concern. He said he would have voted for the legislation if it had been in the House of Lords!

There are two ways of looking at this. The Scottish Executive might be congratulated for making a vital start to land reform without wholly antagonising Scotland's landowners. Or it might be criticised, as it has been by land reform campaigners, for its timidity. After all, there have been demands for 150 years for an era of land reform in Scotland.

But perhaps it is just as important to remember that no serious land reform was on offer before the General Election of 1997, while the changes put before the Holyrood legislature will: make it possible for communities to buy land without fear of foreign bids; end the feudal system; give a right of access to the countryside. Three separate Bills will deal with feudal tenure, the creation of national parks, and the right-to-buy.

Eventually I would like to see a legally enforceable code of land use practice for landowners, a properly funded land bank to help the purchase of property by communities, and an independent environment agency with powers to stop bad practice in nationally important habitats.

For the moment, a start has been made.

Like the store sheep and cattle which are moved out of the Highlands for fattening, so it has been with the children for decades. They move, or are sent, to schools and universities which are thought to offer better opportunity. Beginning to change the way the land is owned and managed must also be about beginning to create new opportunities for people, without damaging wild environments.

Magnus Magnusson once said to me that it was not the charcoal burners or the tanning trade which destroyed the remaining oak forests in Scotland. Indeed, in some instances, these people preserved and looked after the land because it was of value to them; the forests were destroyed when these industries died.

And John Mackenzie of the Assynt Crofters Trust offered hope when he affirmed that he and his colleagues would demonstrate, in future years, the very tangible benefits of communal land ownership, especially in crofting areas, and the value of local residents having control of natural resources.

In 1973, the US Task Force on Land Use Control stated: 'We need to change the policy of allowing property owners to think they can do what they want with their land merely because it's theirs. Owners must come to realise that whatever rights they have in land they happen to own are rights accorded them by society, not rights which they grudgingly permit society to abridge.'

We need to begin to rub out on the land today the unplanned scribblings of the last 300 years. To erase the romantic image perpetrated long ago by Sir Walter Scott, by Edwin Landseer whose *Monarch of the Glen* was commissioned for the House of Lords, and William Scrope, author in 1838 of *The Art of Deer Stalking*.

We have to start to put something back after the regimes of timber, sheep grazing and deerstalking which have been purely extractive. To recognise that we should not be feeding deer in winter, we should be improving their habitat. To admit that we must be doing something wrong when grouse have gone from most of their range since the beginning of the twentieth century, and to tackle the imbalance we have created in the countryside in which the company owning the black forestry block does not work with his neighbour on the grouse moor. To ask why we have allowed red deer numbers to double from 150,000 since 1960.

In 1844, Queen Victoria wrote of a visit to Blair Castle: 'Blair possesses every enjoyment you can desire: shooting, fishing, beautiful scenery . . . and delicious air . . . I am wretched to leave it and we long to return to the dear Highlands which I feel I love . . .'

One hundred and sixty years later, Blair remains an attractive place. The range of shooting it offers, however, has declined, fishings have diminished, the old forests have not produced many new trees, fewer crops are grown, and the estate still makes a loss on its reasonably fertile, schist-base soils. It is much smaller than it was in Queen Victoria's day, and employs fewer people.

The time for land reform is here, change is already happening, and if there are enlightened landowners and managers in Scotland, they will embrace that change.

There is another Scotland within reach, a place where the scenery is greatly enhanced, the wildlife more diverse, the land more fertile and supporting a larger number of people. A place where land-ownership is claimed by many more people and where natural resources are protected by the communities which earn wealth from them.

It is a vision worthy of Scotland. But will the people of Scotland pursue it?

BIBLIOGRAPHY

J.M. Boyd, *Fraser Darling's Islands*, Edinburgh, 1986

J.M. Boyd and I.L. Boyd, *The Hebrides: A Natural History*, London, 1990

Cairngorms Working Party, *Common Sense and Sustainability: A Partnership for the Cairngorms*, Edinburgh 1993

Conroy, Watson, Gunson, *Caring for the High Mountains*, Aberdeen, 1988

R. Crofts, *The Environment – Who Cares?* Occasional Paper No. 2, Scottish Natural Heritage, 1995

F.F. Darling, *Natural History in the Highlands and Islands*, London, 1947 *Wilderness and Plenty: The Reith Lectures*, London, 1969

F.F. Darling and J.M. Boyd, *Natural History in the Highlands and Islands*, London, 1989

S. Gordon, *Highways and Byways in the West Highlands*, London, 1935

J. Hunter, *The Making of the Crofting Community*, Edinburgh, 1991 *The Highlands: A People and their Place*, Edinburgh, 1992 *Towards a Land Reform Agenda for a Scots Parliament*, Rural Forum, Perth, 1995

J. Lister-Kaye, *Ill Fares the Land*, Barail, Skye, 1995

B. MacGregor, *Land Tenure in Scotland*, Rural Forum, Perth, 1993

O. Mackenzie, *A Hundred Years in the Highlands*, Edinburgh, 1988

J. Prebble, *The Highland Clearances*, London, 1969

L. Rich, *Inherit the Land*, London, 1987

Scottish Mountaineering Trust, *Heading for the Scottish Hills*, Glasgow, 1990

T.C. Smout, *A History of the Scottish People 1560–1830*, London, 1985
A Century of the Scottish People 1830–1950, London, 1987
The Highlands and the Roots of Green Consciousness, 1750–1990, Occasional Paper No. 1, Scottish Natural Heritage, 1990

D. Thompson, C. Baxter, *Scotland, Land of Mountains*, Edinburgh, 1995

A. Watson and J. Conroy, *The Cairngorms: Planning Ahead*, Kincardine and Deeside District Council, 1994

M. Wigan, *The Scottish Highland Estate*, Shrewsbury, 1991

A. Wightman, *The Greening of Rural Development*, Scottish Wildlife and Countryside Link, Perth, 1994